Rooted beautifu̶ theology and cu̶̶̶̶ ̶̶̶̶ ̶̶̶̶̶̶̶̶̶̶̶̶ ̶̶̶ contemporary life and challenges. This is a really important read
for any parent raising children in this cultural climate,
any pastor serving a congregation in this social
moment, or any Christian trying to navigate the realities of faithfulness in a complicated time. Stephen
Shaffer does a really nice job bringing to bear the
history of God's people on the challenges of contemporary life, pointing us to our true home, rooted in
Jesus Christ.

— JON BROWN, LEAD PASTOR AT PILLAR
CHURCH (HOLLAND, MI)

I pastor in Seattle, a city full of transplants drawn here
by major tech firms. In this transient culture, people
desire a place to be known and belong. This yearning
points to something deeper that this book pinpoints.
Instead of loneliness and disconnection, we belong to
Jesus. Stephen Shaffer is a pastor who will invite you to
examine your own life and find how the deep
resources of scripture invite you to find home in
Christ.

— DANIEL CLAUS, PASTOR AT
SHORELINE CHRISTIAN REFORMED
CHURCH (SHORELINE, WA)

In *Rooted*, Stephen C. Shaffer addresses the disconnection of the world today and draws the reader's mind and heart back to the seasons of rootedness and rootlessness for the people of Israel. Through the stories of Abraham and Sarah, Esther, the wandering in the wilderness, and others, Shaffer invites us to root our lives in God. This is a timely and compelling book that is sure to challenge and comfort.

— APRIL FIET, PASTOR AT FIRST
PRESBYTERIAN CHURCH OF
SCOTTSBLUFF (SCOTTSBLUFF, NE),
AUTHOR OF *THE SACRED PULSE: HOLY
RHYTHMS FOR OVERWHELMED SOULS*

Reading *Rooted* was an experience of homecoming for me as it connected me again to the story of God's redemption. Shaffer taps deeply into this redemption story by cultivating a biblical metaphor rich enough to hold the seasons of our life with God. May reading *Rooted* be a homecoming for you, too.

— ANDREW MEAD, CO-PASTOR AT
CHURCH OF THE SERVANT CHRISTIAN
REFORMED CHURCH (GRAND
RAPIDS, MI)

Although these current tumultuous times are often described as unprecedented, Stephen Shaffer reminds us that the journey of finding rest and rootedness in God is as old as the story of God's redemptive work in His world. Drawing upon a host of various scenes from scripture, we are assured by Shaffer that the quest for rootedness can take many different paths and can be found in many treasured practices of the Christian faith. In a world of great upheaval, the message found in *Rooted* is one we cannot ignore.

— JOSH VAN LEEUWEN, PASTOR OF
TEACHING AND LEADERSHIP AT
WESTVIEW CHURCH (WAUKEE, IA)

ROOTED

GROWING IN CHRIST IN A ROOTLESS AGE

STEPHEN C SHAFFER

PENIEL PRESS

ROOTED

Growing in Christ in a Rootless Age

Peniel Press

43 Stowe Terrace Brantford, ON N3T 6P2 Canada

www.penielpress.com

Cover design by Angie Koersen

PAPERBACK ISBN: 978-1-7779787-0-9

HARDCOVER ISBN: 978-1-7779787-1-6

EBOOK ISBN: 978-1-7779787-2-3

For Ditty
A genuine hearer and doer of the Word

CONTENTS

INTRODUCTION

It is *rootlessness* and not *meaninglessness* that characterizes the current crisis.

    - Walter Brueggemann

ROOTED

I walked down the lane with my family at my in-laws' farm, on our way to the pond. Rows of freshly planted corn rose on one side and rows of wheat on the other. We chatted about the weather and my father-in-law commented that it was good we had not had too much rain this spring. This seemed odd to me. I always heard farmers talking about needing more rain. I asked (making my best guess) if he was worried about the corn drowning with too much water. Instead, he said, "You need rain in the spring, but if you get too much, the roots won't go very deep. A little dry heat will cause the corn to put its roots deep and make it much stronger later in the year." A little dryness caused the roots to run deeper. As much is true in life with God as in life in the field.

The first Psalm pictures God's people as a tree. "That person is like a tree planted by streams of water, which yields its fruit in season and whose leaf does not wither— whatever they do prospers." (Ps 1:3). The tree is vibrant and strong. Living in North America, I imagined a large pear tree planted next to a bubbling brook. It is full of green leaves year-round, with the juiciest and most delicious pears. This is the Christian life. This is life walking with God, meditating on his word.

When I visited Israel, though, the land where God planted his people, I saw a different picture of Psalm 1. On one outing, we hiked down into what looked like a deserted valley to find nothing but rocks, dry sand, and a couple small, scraggly trees several hundred meters apart. This was a wadi and the trees were acacia trees.

A wadi is a stream that only flows with water occasionally. When it rains in the mountains, the wadi floods and a powerful river flows near this tree. Then it dries up and the acacia tree waits for another rain, for another time when the streams of water flow. Acacia trees are commonly found on the edge of a wadi.

Why do acacia trees thrive in this desert land? Because their roots are deep. You won't find them in nice grasslands where water and rain are abundant, but only in the desert. They are evidence that there is water nearby. You can tell where the wadi floods and where the river flows when you see where the acacia trees are. The land may look dry and parched at the moment, but the acacia tree tells you more than you can see with the naked eye. It tells you where the water flows.

Acacia trees live in a land thirsty for living water. They point to refreshment in a desert where no one can see it. "They are like trees planted by streams of water" (Ps 1:3). God tells us that the righteous — those who walk in right relationship with God — are like acacia trees. They have deep roots – roots that draw in every ounce of moisture and refreshment.

They point those living in a dry and parched land to a place where they can find refreshment. As Jesus said to the Samaritan woman, "If you knew the gift of God and who it is that asks you for a drink, you would have asked him and he would have given you living water." (Jn 4:10) Refreshment, living water, in the desert.

Our life with God is far more like an acacia tree in the wadi than a pear tree by a bubbling brook. We go through periods of dryness and intense heat. We go through the struggles of life in the desert. A friend once confessed to me, with great wisdom, "Sometimes in life with God you are on the mountain peaks and sometimes you are in the valley. When I was younger, I thought that when I was in the valley, there was something wrong with me, that I was somehow unfaithful. As I've grown older, I've learned that this is the normal pattern for our spiritual life. Peaks and valleys. Sometimes this is simply the path God has set us to walk right now. We haven't done anything wrong — we are just called to walk with God in the valley right now." More like an acacia tree in the wadi than a pear tree. However, living in the desert requires deep roots; the acacia survives there because its roots run deep.

The soil of our society is not particularly well-suited for growing deep roots of character and of Christian identity. But has there ever been a time, outside of Eden, when the soil conditions for deep rootedness were ideal? The particular challenges of our time make it difficult to live in a way that draws refreshment from Christ and points others to him. We have immense freedom — to switch jobs, to work remotely, to select schools and even to change churches. People who feel trapped in those places where they were born can, in many instances, move somewhere else. In leaving, they find that God has given them "a wide place for my steps under me, and my feet did not slip" (Ps 18:36). Mobility creates opportunity for many, yet, for others, moving out and moving on means

leaving something behind, even if it cannot be named or iden-
tified. This consistent pattern of uprooting our lives and families for a new job, a new opportunity, or a new church leaves
our roots damaged, our friendships weak, and our souls
drained. We live with more acquaintances, but fewer friends,
because it takes time and proximity for friends and neighbors
to move beyond the surface of shared interests into something
deeper and more meaningful. It takes time to be discipled in a
church. It takes time to feel truly at home in a place. In
moving so much, we struggle to set down roots that will run
deep enough to draw refreshment from Christ when there is
no rain in sight.

The stakes are high, though. A life drawing refreshment
from Christ, bearing fruit that will bless others, is a good, true,
and beautiful life. A life rooted deep in the soil of grace can
withstand the dry seasons of life this side of Eden.

Sadly, there is another way to live — we can live rootless.
We can live without a sense of place in the world, without a
sense of identity in Christ and in his body, the church. We can
live on the surface of things, but there will be consequences.

Why? Because there is another image that appears in Psalm
1: the image of chaff. "Not so the wicked! They are like chaff
that the wind blows away." (Ps 1:4). Chaff is the useless grain
left over from the harvest. At best, it is typically burned. In
ancient times, the practice at harvest was to take all the grain
and throw it into the air. The heavier kernels of grain – the
good stuff – would fall to the ground and be kept, but the
chaff was so light, the wind would catch it and blow it away.
This is how the psalm describes the life of those who walk
apart from God. "They are like chaff that the wind blows
away." (v.4)

The contrast between chaff and the tree is stark. Where the
tree has deep roots and stability, chaff is light and blown away
by the wind. It has no permanence; it ultimately will not

stand. The tree is alive and bearing fruit, but chaff is dead and useless.

Trees and chaff. When applied to our life in Christ, what is the difference between being a tree and being chaff? Between a life rooted in grace, pointing to the refreshment of Jesus Christ, pouring out our lives for others and the life of chaff? How do we become trees when it seems like the rest of the world is chasing after chaff?

The first section of this book wrestles with these very questions. We begin by exploring the gift and challenge of place in the Bible. As people learning to be rooted in a rootless world, we first need to understand how God made us to inhabit our place in this world.

In Chapter 1, we will see how God placed Adam and Eve in the garden of Eden with a mission as wide as the world. The specific place of Eden, with its limits, was a gift from God. For those of us struggling in the modern world, living rooted will mean recovering life as a gift from God and limits as part of that gift.

In Chapter 2, we will walk with the patriarchs as they inhabit the land, but never fully receive it. The land of Israel and the promise of the land form one of the central themes throughout the Bible. The patriarchs walked upon the land, not as a possession, but as a promise. In similar ways, the place we long for with all our hearts is something we receive as a promise from the hand of God. Living rooted means finding our true home in Jesus Christ, who is the fulfillment of the promise of the land, our dwelling place with God.

In Chapter 3, we enter the land of Israel with the people of God. Each tribe and each family was given a plot of land to cultivate and nurture. Through the process of jubilee, a family's place in the land could never be permanently lost. The land of Israel was intended as a school for the people of God to learn how to be *God's* people. They received God's law on

Mount Sinai, but God placed them *in the land* to live out his Word. In the land, they learned community, stability, and love of neighbor. We should remember their example when we are tempted to leave for a different community during hard times; it is in community that we learn to love our neighbors well.

However, in Chapter 4, we will see that living in the land also brings temptation. Simply staying in one place will not make us immune to the temptation to turn from God. In fact, though the people of God grumble and argue with God when they are in the wilderness, they only begin to forget God once they enter the land. Despite its obvious blessings, being rooted in one place also comes with the spiritual temptation to forget God and live as if we made these blessings ourselves. The land is a gift, but it can also be a place of spiritual danger.

As my father-in-law helped me to understand, a little dryness causes the roots to run deeper. When our roots run deep and draw refreshment from the living water, Jesus Christ, we will be able to stand strong in the desert heat and point others to a place where they can find refreshment in Christ.

UPROOTED

A couple years ago, we planted a pear tree in our backyard. We went to the local plant nursery, where we could choose from dozens of healthy trees. Each tree sat in a large plastic flower pot, not in the ground. The trees had been planted from seed, nurtured, grown, tended by the farmers, only to be uprooted from the soil. Each tree began its life in one place, only to be transplanted to another, so that it could bear fruit there.

I took a tree home, dug a hole in the yard, and planted it in our soil. I read about how frequently we needed to water the tree to make sure the roots were awakened and grew strong. Then it hit me: this tree grew up and was rooted deeply in one land, but now made its home in another. Yet, for it to survive, its roots needed to awaken and to burrow deep again. Then it could fulfill its purpose of bearing fruit, but in a new place, for a new people.

The story of scripture is the story of God rooting people deep into the soil. But it is also a story of uprooting. It is a story where God calls people away from places of comfort in order to be planted in new soil. Sometimes God even refuses to let them set down roots, knowing that they will learn to long for the country he has promised. At other times, God pulls up people who are rooted and forcibly transplants them to new lands.

Psalm 1 is our guiding image for section one of the book. We are to be like trees planted by streams of water. With our roots deep in the soil of the land of promise, we are to bear fruit of life with God. There is beauty, challenge, and temptation in being rooted in the land.

But Psalm 1 is not the only story of a tree set by streams of water — the same image shows up in the prophecy of Jeremiah. Jeremiah is a prophet to a crumbling people. His painful, but necessary, calling is to proclaim God's judgment upon his own people. Generations of faithlessness, covenant-breaking, and wickedness — before God and before the world — have withered the nation. King after king has left the nation in tatters. Jeremiah is called to proclaim that God will bring judgment upon the people, destruction to Jerusalem and the temple, and cast the people into seventy years of exile. And Jeremiah, despite his faithfulness, is to go along with the people into that exile.

In chapter 17, Jeremiah says that Judah's sins have become deeply ingrained. "Judah's sin is engraved with an iron tool, inscribed with a flint point, on the tablets of their hearts and on the horns of their altars" (Jer 17:1). Sin has covered the land and become a permanent fixture in their hearts. It is for this reason that they will enter into exile. "Through your own fault you will lose the inheritance I gave you. I will enslave you to your enemies in a land you do not know, for you have kindled my anger and it will burn forever" (Jer 17:4).

The chapter then takes a turn that parallels the negative path laid out in Psalm 1. Those who refuse to place their trust in the Lord find condemnation. However, unlike in the psalm, they are not compared to chaff that is blown away, but to a dry fruitless bush in the desert.

> This is what the LORD says:
> "Cursed is the one who trusts in man,
> Who draws strength from mere flesh
> And whose heart turns away from the LORD.
> That person will be like a bush in the wastelands;
> They will not see prosperity when it comes.
> They will dwell in the parched places of the desert,
> In a salt land where no one lives (Jer 17:5-6)

What is true of chaff is also true of the bush. A life lived apart from God is fruitless. Yet, unlike chaff, which is dead and has no roots, those Jeremiah speaks of are firmly rooted in their trust in themselves and their own effort. They are rooted, but not in the Lord. They are planted with roots, but in soil that does not bring life. Like the Israelites, we can be rooted, too, but in the wrong place.

Following the path of Psalm 1, Jeremiah then speaks of those who trust in God:

> But blessed is the one who trusts in the LORD,
> whose confidence is in him.
> They will be like a tree planted by the water
> That sends out its roots by the stream.
> It does not fear when heat comes;

Its leaves are always green.
It has no worries in a year of drought
And never fails to bear fruit (Jer 17:7-9)

Jeremiah 17 follows almost exactly the same pattern as Psalm 1, but the context is different. Those who trust in the Lord are planted by streams, have deep roots, and bear fruit, even when the land is dry. There is a strength, permanence, and blessedness to all who trust in the Lord. Their life bears fruit for the blessings of the world around them and the glory of God. While there is shared imagery between Psalm 1 and Jeremiah 17, Psalm 1 imagines us being planted by streams in the land of Israel, rooted in the land of promise — Jeremiah 17 gives us no such illusions.

Jeremiah's cries are words to a people entering exile, people who will be uprooted from the land of Israel and carried off into a foreign land. For generations, they have been firmly rooted in the land of Israel, but not in the God of Israel. They have been like that dry bush in the wilderness, stuck in one place, but bearing no fruit. Though the exile is God's judgment on the people, it is also God's intentional act of transplanting people so that they might find their true roots again in God and come to bear fruit.

The rootlessness of our culture can often manifest itself in a kind of aimlessness. It is a journey without a destination, a movement for the sake of movement. "The sense of being lost, displaced, and homeless is pervasive in contemporary culture. The yearning to belong somewhere, to have a home, to be in a safe place, is a deep and moving pursuit."[1] We resist this restless wandering by recovering a biblical sense of place and the land in the Christian life. There is a biblical form of rootlessness as well. The people of God are not always called to stay where they are, but are moved by God.

God roots people deep into the land of promise, but God

also uproots people so that they can bear fruit for his kingdom. In order to understand how to be rooted in Christ in a rootless land, we will look closely at those times where God does not simply let people stay where they are, but uproots them for their good and the glory of his name. Sometimes being rooted in Christ involves uprooting our life to follow where he leads.

In Chapter 5, we will walk with Abraham as he leaves behind everything he has ever known to follow God. He is uprooted and brought to the land of Canaan, but even there he is never quite at home. Abraham and his descendants live with a kind of rootlessness. In every place they are vulnerable, their status and relationship to the broader culture and powers unsure. They consistently run the risk of being exploited and of enduring injustice. God continues to uproot his people in order to plant them in new places. When we trust God's promise more than the security the world can offer, we can join Abraham in following where God leads.

In Chapter 6, we take our cues from Israel's time in the wilderness. The wilderness times for Israel are periods of difficulty and grumbling, but also of intimacy with God. God refuses to leave Israel rooted in Egypt, for it is a land of death. He rescues them with his mighty hand and then spends 40 years teaching them to hunger and thirst for him instead of for their old life in Egypt. In Egypt, rootedness is death and being uprooted is salvation. The wilderness is a place of struggle, rebellion, and ultimately meeting with the holy presence of God. Uprooting is part of the story of God's salvation.

In Chapter 7, we see God uprooting the people from the land itself and sending them into exile in Babylon. The exile creates a crisis of faith, forcing Israel to learn how to live as God's people in a foreign land.

In the 21st century, we live in what David Kinnaman and Mark Matlock call "Digital Babylon." "It is the pagan-but-spiritual, hyper-stimulated, multicultural, imperial crossroads that is the virtual home of every person with Wi-Fi, a data plan, or — for most of us — both."[2] Israel and the church face different temptations in Babylon than in the land of Israel. Digital Babylon requires developing a resilient faith so that we can be rooted in Christ despite the growing pressures of the world around us.

In Chapter 8, we see how God uses his transplanted people as a vehicle to spread the gospel. God's scattered people become the staging ground for the mission of the church. Synagogues become the first stops on every missionary tour. The lessons of resilience learned in the exile are carried into the missionary world of the early Church. The people of God live as those who belong to God and never fully belong to the land they lived in. This resilient faith and scattering of the people combines for the massive spread of the gospel in the early Church. Being uprooted can make mission messy, but can also carry both opportunity and conflict in its wake.

The pear tree in my backyard did not begin its life there. It was not nurtured from a seed a few feet from my back fence. Yet, it is *there* that it will bear fruit for years to come. Uprooted from its native soil, it was transplanted to my yard so that my family would enjoy the sweetness of its fruit. Where God plants us might not be where we started. Some of us might be called to grow in our native soil, but others will be transplanted to places near and far in order to bear fruit so that others can taste the sweetness of Christ. May the living water of the word awaken our roots so that they might burrow deep again into the soil where God has planted us.

FINDING HOME

Where is home? Is it the land of promise or the wilds of exile? Are we meant to deepen our roots into the soil of the local or be ready at any time to be uprooted for the sake of God's kingdom?

Our home is in Jesus Christ. The fulfillment of the land of promise is none other than Jesus Christ. The early Church, like Israel, grieved at the fall and destruction of the second temple in 70 AD. The center of the land, the center of worship, had been destroyed. Yet, as Michael Horton points out, the temple's destruction did not put the church in crisis because the center of worship, the center of our hope for life with God, had already been found in Jesus Christ. "The early Christian reaction to the destruction of the temple was not to look for a third one, with a revived Sinaitic theocracy, but to look to Christ as the reality to which these earthly institutions pointed."[3] Worship found its center in Jesus. "From now on, true worship will be determined not by any religious edifice, but by whether it takes place in Jesus Christ as the holy place."[4] Our identity and our life find their center in Jesus. He is our home and our true land. Thus, whether we are called to remain where we are or whether we are called to uproot our lives and be transplanted to another place, we have not left home when we are in Christ. Jesus himself says, in John 15:

I am the true vine, and my Father is the vinegrower. He removes every branch in me that bears no fruit. Every branch that bears fruit he prunes to make it bear more fruit. You have already been cleansed by the word that I have spoken to you. Abide in me as I abide in you. Just as the branch cannot bear fruit by itself unless it abides in the vine, neither can you unless you abide in me. I am the vine, you are the branches. Those who abide in me and I in them bear much fruit, because apart from me you can do nothing. Whoever does not abide in me is thrown away like a branch and withers; such branches are gathered, thrown into the fire, and burned. If you abide in me, and my words abide in you, ask for whatever you wish, and it will be done for you. My Father is glorified by this, that you bear much fruit and become my disciples. As the Father has loved me, so I have loved you; abide in my love. If you keep my commandments, you will abide in my love, just as I have kept my Father's commandments and abide in his love. I have said these things to you so that my joy may be in you, and that your joy may be complete. (15:1-11 NRSV).

To "abide in Christ" is to make our abode in Christ, to make our home in him.[5] In the Incarnation, God the Son took on flesh and made his abode with us, he "lived among us" (Jn 1:14). At the end of all things, the dwelling place of God will be with mortals (Rev 21:2). God will be our God and we will be his people. That ultimate dwelling place is physical, but it is also always and ever in Jesus Christ. More than any acreage or neighborhood or city center, Jesus Christ is our true home.

This does not discount the importance of place or caring for the land and people in our midst. Far from it. However, it does put all our earthly longings in their proper place. "The soul's hunger for peace is a longing for a kind of rest from anxiety and frantic pursuits — it is to rest in God."[6] The longing for home, for place, for rootedness is ultimately a longing for Jesus. However good all the homes and places we live may be, we will remain restless until we learn to rest in Jesus Christ. "As our attention is moved from our resources, our self-made homes apart from Christ, and we direct our hearts to Christ by the Spirit in worship, we encounter, hear, taste, and see our true identity as children of the Father."[7]

While the first two sections of the book explore the biblical themes of land and exile, the third section focuses on the call to abide in Christ, to make our home in him. In five chapters, this section examines five practices in the life of the

church that enable us to live more deeply in our true home in
Jesus Christ.

In Chapter 9, we explore the rich symbolism contained in
both circumcision and baptism and the deep connection
between the two practices. In both, the people of God are cut
off from the world in order to be brought into the people
of God.

In Chapter 10, we join Abraham at Mamre as he mourns
the death of Sarah and buries her. Christian funerals and practices of mourning enable us to face the harsh reality of death
and to hold fast to the hope of the gospel. Additionally, we
will see how the Christian funeral, like Mamre before it, is a
down payment on the promise of the final resurrection and
thus a place of profound gospel hope.

In Chapter 11, we join Israel in exile as they receive God's
gift of the book of psalms. In order to maintain our identity in
a foreign land, God gave us a prayer and song book. By singing
and praying the psalms, God's people learn to bring all of their
life before God and to receive their life from him.

In Chapter 12, we join Israel around the table at the feasts.
By giving Israel a series of seven feasts, God reorients their time
around his saving work and not their achievement or effort.
Additionally, these feasts are meals with God and with one
another. The fulfillment of these feasts is found in the sacrament of the Lord's Supper. The Supper is God's gift to
reorient our lives around his saving acts and a feast of communion with God and with one another.

In the final chapter, we will explore the role of wisdom for
God's people living in exile. Looking at the lives of Joseph,
Esther, and Daniel, we will see how wisdom shaped them to
know when to say "yes" and when to say "no" to the culture
around them. This wisdom enables a confident witness, even
when it leads to suffering.

Where is home? In a rootless world, we long for a place

where we find peace, rest, and belonging. We long for a place where we are known, loved, and even challenged to live more fully. This longing, and God's promises, change how we relate to our current homes, our physical neighborhoods, and our fast-paced, digital world. My hope through this book is that you will grow more at home in the one who is your true home, Jesus Christ.

ROOTED

They are like trees planted by streams of water,
Which yield their fruit in its season,
And their leaves do not wither.
In all that they do, they prosper.
Psalm 1:3 NRSV

1

THE GIFT OF PLACE

THE GARDEN OF EDEN

Man's limit is in the middle of his existence, not on the edge.
- Dietrich Bonhoeffer

This was God's perfect plan: the people of God in the place of God dwelling in the presence of God.
- Sandra L. Richter

When we see life as it is supposed to be, we realize how far away we are. Growing up in two different homes, I always had a sense that things were not as they should be. I knew God's intention for marriage was to get married, have kids, and stay together forever. I knew it, but I lived between two homes and two sets of parents, with my feet in two families. I do not remember my parents being married, nor the time before they both had remarried. Though all four of my parents were loving, godly people who loved me and gave me a stable home, I often felt uncertain about my place, about where I truly belonged. I am not trying to judge my parents. I am simply recognizing that I lived with unsure footing that I struggled to name or identify.

Then I met my wife and saw her come home and interact with her family. Seeing a family that was whole helped me identify the ache in my soul. Seeing more clearly what families were made for enabled me to name the longing in my own heart.

In order to know what we have lost, we need to know where we began. We need to know what we were meant for. We need to know where God has placed us and our purpose in that place. We need to know Eden in order fully to understand our life outside of it.

In Eden, God sets Adam and Eve down into a specific place full of abundance and purpose. God provides them with the gift of life, as well as limits that are important for life with God. Yet, despite all these blessings, our first parents trusted the serpent's lies over God and cast themselves and us to wander outside of the garden.

SET DOWN IN THE GARDEN

In the opening chapter of the Bible, God speaks the world into existence. At his word, stars come into the sky, the waters pull back, and mountains jut up from the earth. At his command, the sun and moon are set in the sky, the earth bursts forth with plants, and the fish, birds, and beasts begin to swim, to slither, and to roam. In six days, God forms the earth and fills it.

God creates space and then fills it. On the first day, he separates light and dark, creating day and night. On the fourth day, he sets the sun and moon over the day and the night (Gen 1:3-5, 14-19). He separates the waters on day two, creating space for oceans and sky, then fills it with fish and birds on the fifth day (1:6-8, 20-23). He gathers the waters on the third day, revealing dry ground and covering it with seed-bearing vegetation, then fills the ground with livestock, beasts, and creeping things on the sixth day (1:9-13, 24-25). There is a consistent pattern in the days of creation. God creates space and then fills it.

On the sixth day, God creates man and woman in his image (1:26-27). He sets Adam and Eve down in the garden as their home. God creates this space and gives it to them; now it is their responsibility to fill it. "God blessed them and said to them, "Be fruitful and increase in number; fill the earth and subdue it. Rule over the fish in the sea and the birds in the sky and over every living creature that moves on the ground"" (1:28). This man and woman, these image-bearers, are to guard and to guide all the living creatures of creation, to lead them in a resounding chorus of praise to God (Ps 19:1). They are God's representatives on earth, working as stewards of the riches of creation under God's ultimate authority.[1] God creates humankind and gives them a blessing and a task that stretches as wide as creation itself.

Genesis 2 tells a narrower and more intimate creation story, zooming in on the formation of Adam and Eve. This compliments rather than contradicts the wide-angle view of Genesis 1. God draws near to create a man in his image. "Then the Lord God formed a man from the dust of the ground and breathed into his nostrils the breath of life, and the man became a living being." (Gen 2:7). The Spirit that hovered at creation (1:3) now fills Adam's nostrils, bringing life.

Then God sets Adam down in a garden. God creates this garden as a home for joy and flourishing, as a place of belonging. Adam is called to fill and rule the whole creation, but his life and his calling begins in Eden. He does not start in no man's land, though. He does not begin lost and wandering. In Eden, Adam has a place where he belongs.

God provides a place for Adam. "Now the Lord God had planted a garden in the east, in Eden; and there he put the man he had formed" (2:8). Adam never has to find himself or search out a place to lay his head. Instead, Adam begins belonging. He begins with his feet firmly rooted in the soil of Eden. His calling could and likely would have brought him to the ends of the earth, but he begins already rooted.

PLACE VERSUS SPACE

God made us to live in a place. *Place*, however, is about more than mere physical space. It is something we receive, something to which we belong, something that shapes us. We must live in physical space, but we are meant to live belonging to a *place*. As Walter Brueggemann points out, there is a huge difference between "space" and "place."

> "Space" means an arena of freedom, without coercion or accountability, free of pressures and void of authority. Space may be imaged as weekend, holiday, avocation, and is characterized by a kind of neutrality or emptiness waiting to be filled by our choosing. Such a concern appeals to a desire to get out from under meaningless routine and subjection. But "place" is a very different matter. Place is space that has historical meanings, where some things have happened that are now remembered and that provide continuity and identity across generations. Place is space in which important words have been spoken that have established identity, defined vocation, and envisioned destiny.[2]

While space is important, what we really hunger for is *place*. We long for somewhere to belong, to know who we are, and to know our calling. In Genesis 1, God creates space in order to fill it with purpose and order. In Genesis 2, God sets Adam and Eve down in a *place*.

Space is something that we shape and fashion, but place is also something that shapes and fashions us. Space can be whatever we want it to be. Place constrains us and yet causes us to flourish. Space is the kind of rootlessness that happens when we live somewhere flitting on the surface, never risking putting down roots. Jesus warns that such a life without roots in him will soon wither (Jn 15:6).

We live in a culture that idolizes the freedom of space. In Digital Babylon, we can be everywhere and nowhere at the same time. Our technology promises us a kind of connection and relationship separated from place, cut off from physical space. We can connect with people on Twitter or Facebook on the other side of the globe, join in on Zoom calls with colleagues on the other side of the country, and collaborate in real-time, all from the comfort of our homes. We can live anywhere and never lose our digital connections or our online community. We can be connected to more people than any generation before and yet be more lonely.

How can we be lonely when we have "friends" around the world? How can we be lonely when we are more "connected" than we have ever been? Because we lack a sense of place—we are rootless. Rootlessness leads to loneliness because space does not deliver on its promises. We are promised we can "lead detached, unrooted lives of endless choice and no commitments,"[3] but only find ourselves more exhausted, isolated, and miserable than ever before. When we are everywhere and nowhere at the same time, we find life wearying. We can be connected with people across the globe, but disconnected from the place where we live and the people who surround us.

The advent of COVID-19 has only accelerated a trend that already existed as a result of our ever-increasing access to information technology. Many of us spent a year or more working or learning from home. With a few clicks, we could change our Zoom background to pretend we were anywhere, but pretending quickly grew old. Because we could be anywhere, it didn't matter *where* we were. *Place* — the walking path, the local coffee shop, the rolling hills and bubbling rivers

— shrank down to mere *space*. We needed more packages on the front steps, or another backyard project to try to bring order to the chaos of life.

We might imagine that being forced to spend large amounts of time at home with our families would lead to greater connection and greater rootedness, but many of us found the opposite to be true. Though we could move and travel less, we also became less connected to the place where God had set us down. The less we got out and moved, the more we felt the ground shifting under our feet.[4] The more time we spent at home, the less connected we were to *where* we were. Our roots shriveled in front of a screen.

LONGING FOR EDEN

We still long for Eden, for the place God made for us. He formed the man from the dust, breathed life into his nostrils, and set him down in a garden. Eden had geography. The land was watered by a river, which flowed from the garden into four headwaters: the Pishon, Gihon, Tigris, and Euphrates. Adam and Eve walked with God in the garden (Gen 3:8). They knew its trees, its hills, and what it was like to walk with God in this place. In Eden, our first parents not only knew where they were, but who they were. There was work to be done in the garden (2:15), but this work had not yet become toil. The purpose of their work was never frustrated. The ground did not produce thorns and thistles, but only trees that were pleasing to the eye and good for food (2:9). Our first parents were set down into a place overflowing with the abundant goodness of God. We long to return to Eden.

Place also involves not only God's abundant goodness, but involves community. From the very beginning, God made human beings for relationship with one another. Husbands and wives, parents and children, friends and neighbors.

In Genesis 1, everything is good and, ultimately, it is "very good" (1:31). However, in Adam's isolation, suddenly something is 'not good.' "It is not good for the man to be alone. I will make a helper suitable for him" (2:18). God brings all the beasts of the field and the birds of the air before Adam, but no suitable helper is found. God causes him to fall into a deep sleep, takes one of his ribs, and forms a woman — the bone of his bones and flesh of his flesh. "The man and his wife were both naked, and they felt no shame" (2:25). Adam and Eve are made for each other, to be in deep relationship with one another.

I don't think this nakedness is merely a lack of clothing. To be naked is to be exposed, vulnerable, and intimate, where nothing is hidden. This is the relationship Adam and Eve have in the garden. They are both naked and feel no shame. Theirs is a relationship of intimacy and vulnerability, where nothing is hidden. "In addition to this perfect place, Adam and Eve are given each other (Gen 2:18-25), and, as is implied in Genesis 3:8, they are given full access to their loving Creator."[5]

We are made for this, too. We are made for intimacy, trust, and vulnerability with no shame. Adam and Eve also regularly stood naked before God — physically, emotionally, spiritually. Trusting, intimate, transparent, unashamed. This is *place*, where we are rooted and belong so we can grow into the mission God has placed before us. "This was God's perfect plan: the *people* of God in the *place* of God dwelling in the *presence* of God."[6]

We long for place. We long to return to Eden, not simply as a space without all the damning and destructive effects of sin, but also as a place where we belong. We ache for Eden because we were made to be rooted in the land, to flourish where God has set us down. We were made for a mission as wide as creation, but to live out that mission with our feet firmly planted in the soil, where God has placed us. "God prepares an exceedingly beautiful garden for man, whom he has created with his own hands. And what will the man of the desert think of but a land with beautiful streams and trees full of fruit?"[7] As people born on the far side of Eden, we long for its rivers and trees, we long to sink our bare feet into its soil, we long for a place where we know not just where we are, but who we are, and what we were made for. We are made, not for space, but for place.

In a shifting world, where the ground feels like it changes from day to day, we ache for Eden, for a place where we can set down roots and grow. But, as we will see, we cannot go back to Eden. The way is barred by the flaming sword of the Cherubim. The only way home will be through the desert.

LIFE FROM THE CENTER

The man is not all that God places in the garden. "In the middle of the garden were the tree of life and the tree of the knowledge of good and evil" (2:9). God places two trees at the center of the garden. Though the garden is full of fruit-bearing trees, these two trees are singled out. Pastor and theologian Dietrich Bonhoeffer argues these two trees point to the gift of life and to the gift of limits at the center of our lives.

First, there is the tree of life. Life is a gift to be received from the hands of God, not an achievement to be earned. Adam and Eve would have been free to eat from this tree. It is only after having eaten from the tree of knowledge that they are forbidden to eat from the tree of life. "Before this, life was not problematic nor was it something to be pursued or seized. It was there, given, life in the presence of God."[8] The presence of the tree of life in the middle speaks to a fundamental theological truth: God is the source of our life and God is at the center. Adam and Eve did not give themselves life. They did not fight and scrape for life, but received it from the hands of

God. "Adam's life comes from the middle which is not Adam himself but God."[9] The tree at the center points to God at the center of our life and existence. In the tree of life, God gives us life as a gift.

Even exiled from Eden, our life is a gift to be received, not an accomplishment to earn. We are radically dependent creatures. In the womb, we depend upon our mother for everything: food, warmth, shelter, connection, safety. From our first breath, we depend on others to feed us, to clothe us, and to shelter us. We must be taught to walk, to read, and to speak. Though we grow in strength and agency, we never outgrow this dependence. We wear clothes sewn by others, eat food grown by others, and drive cars made by others. There are no truly self-made men and women. Under and behind this very human dependence upon each other, however, is a greater and more fundamental dependence upon God. At the center of the garden was the tree of life. At the center of our lives is the gift of life. "The life that comes forth from God is in the middle. That means that God, who gives life, is in the middle."[10] Recovering life as a gift is one way of recovering God at the center of life.

Our life is a gift from the hands of God. God's gift of life sat in the center of the garden and his gift of life should sit at the center of our lives. This is what we long for when we long for place, when we long for roots. We ache for the Edenic life where life is a gift from God and where we live in the presence of God. Adam has this life "just because he lives from the middle of life and on the strength of the middle of life but he himself does not live in the middle."[11] Living life from God and in the presence of God requires that we live *from* the middle without putting ourselves *in* the middle. We must live with our center in God without putting ourselves in the center.

The tree of life is a visible sign of God's invisible grace.

sacramental

God's grace and care, which sustains all of creation, puts breath in Adam's lungs, causes the sun to shine, and causes the land to bring forth fruit, is made tangible in the tree of life. God's sustaining grace at the center of life is made visible with the tree at the center of the garden. Adam and Eve taste the goodness of God in the fruit of the tree of life.

Outside of Eden, we do not have access to this tree. The way is barred for us back into Eden. However, we can still taste and see the goodness of God. We have been given a visible sign and seal of God's grace and goodness to us in the bread and wine of the Lord's Supper. At the Supper, we find our center in God and not in ourselves. In the bread and cup, we feast upon Christ, who is our life. We receive true life as a gift at the Table. Though the way to the tree of life is barred, the Table is set for us.

THE LIMIT IS IN THE MIDDLE

There is another tree in the center of the garden. The tree of the knowledge of good and evil stands as a gracious limit upon Adam and Eve's freedom. "And the LORD God commanded the man, "You are free to eat from any tree in the garden; but you must not eat from the tree of the knowledge of good and evil, for when you eat from it you will certainly die" (Gen 2:16-17). Limits are a part of living in the garden. Being rooted in the place God has set us, living life from God and in the presence of God, we are confronted with our limits. There are certain things we cannot do, lines we cannot cross, things we cannot taste and still live from this center of life with God.

There is a 'yes' and a 'no' at the center of the garden. There is the 'yes' of life as a gift from God, the tree of life given freely in the center of the garden, pointing to God as the center of our life. Yet, there is also a 'no.' We must not eat from *that* tree. The knowledge of good and evil is reserved for God alone and is not for us to have.

Living within limits is to live as a creature. "This man, who is addressed as the one who is free, is shown his limit, that is to say, his creatureliness."[12] Freedom in the garden is not the freedom of autonomy or unlimited choice, a mere freedom from restraint, but instead freedom *for* life with God. It is the freedom that comes from being rooted in place, being rooted in Christ who remains at the center. Adam is free, but free precisely as a he observes the limits God has given. It is the freedom not to seek to be the Creator, but to live as a creature. To be a free creature is to live *as* a creature.

We cannot do everything. We cannot be everywhere. Part of the rootlessness of our age stems from our attempts to deny our limits of time and space. Technology and the stories we tell ourselves around it, have led us to believe that we can be present anywhere, at any time, with the push of a button. "What we hardly ever want to admit is that we are limited creatures. Subject to the confines of time and space, we cannot be anywhere, anytime. As a matter of fact, we can only be in this place, now."[13]

Yet, the more alienated we are from the limits of what it means to be human, the more we push ourselves to the center and cut ourselves off from the tree of life. "Our desire to get out of the limits of time is, at root, a desire to become like God by our own efforts. This is what the Christian tradition calls sin."[14] Living rooted is an invitation to live with the limits that come with being a creature, as well as the specific limits given by God in his Word.

This limit is not at the edge of the garden, but at the center. We like to think of limits at the boundaries, like fences we can choose to hop over or break through. We look at limits and wonder how easily we could surpass them. Our body aches? Take this supplement. Wrinkles? Try this cream. Not enough time in the day? Try this life hack. Yet, this denial of limits is not a path to freedom, but to slavery. All the workout routines, vitamin supplements, or skin-care products in the world (as good and useful as they may be) will not prevent us from eventually dying. Post-Eden, death is a limit we cannot cross. The obsession with extending life, while not bad in itself, can become a brutal master. No amount of life hacks, time-saving tips, or delegation will add one more hour to our day. These are boundaries within which we must live. To accept limits is to enter into freedom. To deny them is to invite frustration and exhaustion. We ache to push boundaries, yet God places the tree of the knowledge of good and evil in the center of the garden.

There are two trees in the center of the garden. The tree of life points to God's gift of life and to God at the center of life. The tree of the knowledge of good and evil points to the limits at the center of human life. We can only accept one by accepting the other. We can only receive life as a gift from God when we accept the limits that also lie at the center of life with God. God is God and we are not. Some things God has given us and some things he has said are not for us.

These limits are gifts from God. As J. Todd Billings says,

> Don't *deny* your weakness or the frailty of your mortal state, acting as if you could command the material world to bend to your will. Instead, delight in what is beautiful, be grateful for each day, and expect trouble ("Today's trouble is enough for today"). Take joy in the daily gifts of the Creator. But remember that you won't make it out of this journey alive. Use each day's strength to seek the temple, the kingdom, and the King.[15]

Living rooted requires recovering limits at the center of our life. Though the whole world was the theatre of their mission, Adam and Eve were set down by God in a particular place, the garden. In the center of that garden were two trees, visible and tangible signs of two realities at the center of life. Life is a gift that comes from the hand of God and yet that life comes with limits. Living with both the gift of life and limits at the center is a way of recovering God at the center of life.

FLEEING AND WANDERING

Obviously, we no longer live in Eden. We see it in a world where lives are cheaply taken while cameras roll. We see it in a world filled with exploitation and injustice, where the strong so frequently abuse rather than protect. We see it in a world of disembodied rage or virtue signaling on social media, where advocacy and love are cut off from neighbors and projected onto a screen. In myriad ways, we know what has happened. We were made for place, belonging, and for mission, to be rooted where we are so that we can grow in God's kingdom mission. We were made for life centered in God, in the good gift of life from God and in the presence of God. We were made to live with limits and, in doing so, find freedom for life with God.

Even if we didn't have the story of Genesis 3, we would know somewhere deep in our souls that something has gone wrong. Creation that was designed to soar with Adam and Eve at the helm has been thrown into a tailspin. Having had a glimpse of Eden, of the place we were meant to be, we feel our alienation all the more deeply. As Chuck DeGroat puts it, "We can only grasp the doctrine of original sin (that sin has infected everything and everyone) if we first grasp original goodness (that we were all created good and in God's image)."[16] The goodness of Eden sharpens the pain of exile.

Adam and Eve are not content with the limit at the center of their lives. Through the coaxing of the serpent, they mistrust God's promise and his goodness and take the fruit from the one tree from which God commanded them not to partake. The serpent promises that they will be like God. As Bonhoeffer says, "[Adam] has transgressed the limit and now he hates his limit, he denies it, he is like God, without a limit."[17] Instead of being like God, they find shame and alienation. They disobey the single, direct command of God and send all of creation careening off course. The relationship of intimacy is shattered. Shame, guilt, pain, distance, and brokenness enter the picture.

The theological word for what happened is 'sin.' In their sin, Adam and Eve are cut off from God, cut off from each other, cut off from themselves, and eventually are exiled from their place, cast out of Eden. Through Adam and Eve's disobedience, all of the good creation that they were called to steward was affected. They fell. We fell. All of creation fell. Our best theologians would say that every area of our lives has been affected. We are born into a world broken and fallen and we contribute to this fallenness ourselves. We begin our life already uprooted, searching for home, searching for our place. We are born outside the garden with the cherubim guarding the way back and our hearts aching for entry.

Adam and Eve's first reaction is to hide. "Then the eyes of both of them were opened, and they realized they were naked, so they sewed fig leaves together and made coverings for themselves" (Gen 3:7). We are still hiding. We are experts at sewing fig leaves. Fig leaves to hide our mistakes, to hide our failures, to hide our fears, to hide our very selves. We are still running and hiding from each other, and we are still, like Adam and Eve, afraid of and hiding from God.

Adam and Eve run and hide, but God does not let them stay hiding. "Man is not allowed to remain in his sin alone, God speaks to him, he stops him in his flight."[18] We run from God, but God still seeks us out. After Adam and Eve hear God and hide among the trees, God calls to them, "Where are you?" God seeks those in hiding. He seeks Adam and Eve, calls them out of hiding. God knows where they are, but in seeking them, he calls them out of hiding and to himself. We hide, but God seeks us in our hiddenness.

In their confession, Adam and Eve continually pass the blame. Adam blames Eve. Eve blames the serpent. Even in their confession, they hide and run. Even before they are sent out of the garden, they have already become rootless, they are already disconnected from their place and their calling. While necessary, the exit from Eden only reveals what was true the moment they ate the fruit.

God then pronounces a curse with which we still live. The snake will eat dust, but will one day be crushed. Intimacy will be twisted by power struggles. The womb that brings life will also bring pain. The work that was meant to flourish will be frustrated. The ground will produce thorns and thistles and, "by the sweat of your brow you will eat your food until you return to the ground" (Gen 3:19).

In her book, *The Epic of Eden: A Christian Entry into the Old Testament*, Sandra Richter gives insight into the phrase 'by the sweat of our brow.' She says, contrary to what we might first think, the phrase has nothing to do with hard work. Instead,

> this idiom speaks of anxiety — perspiration-inducing *fear*. Where does anxiety fit into God's curse upon us? What we find in Genesis 3 is that because of the rebellion of the earth and the expulsion of Adam and Eve from God's presence, humanity will now live their lives in an adversarial world with a constant, gnawing undercurrent of dread that there will not be enough, that their labor will not meet the need. What if the crop fails? The livestock die? A fire, storm, or drought? Can you relate? What about groceries this week?

Rent, mortgage and car payment? College tuition? Retirement? What if I get sick? What if my kids get sick?...This is the curse...limited resources, an insecure future and a world that no longer responds to my commands. Any Adams out there?[19]

One of the forms our rootlessness takes is gnawing dread and perspiration-inducing fear. Our lives are marked by endless toil, gripping fear, and the terror that all our efforts will never be enough. We seek to claw our way back into the garden, back to place and stability and home, back to a sense of where we are and who we are. We might pursue "technique" as a way back — we need the right planner, the right system, the right team and then we will finally be okay. If we just learn this hack or start this habit, we can get life back on the right track. We might pursue "hustle" as the path back to Eden, pushing hour after hour, week after week, year after year, promising ourselves that when we finally crest the next ridge, then we can rest, then we will be safe. But the race never stops.

The story of Adam and Eve's abandonment of their mission and their exile from Eden could have been the end of the story altogether. Yet, God is gracious and patient. Our first parents move outside the garden, the only kind of life they have ever known. They bear two sons, Cain and Abel. They grow and eventually present offerings to God. Abel's pleases God, while Cain's does not (Gen 4:4-5). Cain grows angry. God warns Cain this anger could easily lead to sin. Cain brushes God off and invites his brother, Abel, out to the field, where Cain kills him. It is easier to hate his brother, to kill his brother, than to deal with God and himself. Violence is more expedient than repentance. It is simpler to be angry with Abel for doing well than to recognize his own failures.

Adam and Eve bear a son who seizes death instead of life.

They eat from the tree of knowledge that promises to bring death and are denied the tree of life. Now, Cain carries death, not life, in his hands. As Bonhoeffer says, "The man who is not allowed to eat of the tree of life all the more greedily reaches out for the fruit of death, the destruction of life."[20] After killing Abel, God confronts Cain with a chance to come clean. Cain dodges God and is banished from the land. We do not know whether Cain's heart is ever softened or whether God's grace in protecting him changes him at all. Cain leaves the Lord's presence as a wanderer.

We often find ourselves wandering along with Cain, east of Eden. We were made for life in the presence of God, dwelling in the place where God has set us down. But we find our hearts, our lives, and our very bodies wandering upon the earth. We cannot seem to settle, to find our place, to set down roots in the good soil.

Is this restless life all we can ever hope for? No. God promises that he will one day make a different ending. Fallen creation, and fallen people exiled from Eden, long for the coming of Christ. "Christ on the Cross, the murdered Son of God, is the end of the story of Cain, and thus the actual end of the story."[21] Genesis 3 and 4, which has been a continuous downward spiral, ends with a note of hope. "At that time people began to call on the name of the Lord" (Gen 4:26). Bare and restless, some people turn, not back toward the land of Eden, but toward the Lord. "The tree of life, the Cross of Christ, the middle of the fallen and preserved world of God, for us that is the end of the story of paradise."[22]

FROM EDEN TO THE PROMISE

By contemplating Eden, we realize how far we have gone from where we belong. We are made not just to inhabit space, but to be rooted in a place. Place is where we know *where* we are and *who* we are because we live from God and in the presence of God. Adam and Eve were called to steward the whole earth, but were placed in the specific location of Eden. In the middle of the garden were two trees, which point to two central facts at the center of life. In the tree of life, we see life as a gift to be received from the hand of God. In the tree of knowledge of good and evil, we see limitations as gifts for living life with God. Yet, we see that Adam and Eve rejected this calling, trusted the serpent and sent themselves (and all their children) out of Eden, wandering with no prospect of return.

We were meant for Eden. God created us to live with him, in deep intimate relationship with him. We were meant to live from our center in God and not in ourselves. We were made to be rooted in our physical space, living within our limits as a gift. We were made to receive life as a gift from God.

But we do not live in Eden. We cannot return. Yet, God has not abandoned us. God still gives us his good gifts — place, limits, a center in God. But now, east of Eden, we must be rooted in God in the midst of the pain and suffering of sin. The promise of God's redemption is to find our true home in God. The story of God making right what went wrong in the garden must, however, go through the wilderness before we can finally come home.

As we move out from Eden, we enter a time where land is promised, but not yet given. Abraham, Isaac, Jacob, and his sons live hearing God's promise to bring them into a land, but they have not received it yet. They cling to land as a promise.

2

THE PROMISE OF HOME

HOPING WITH THE PATRIARCHS

To an observer, the sojourner-pilgrim is just there, coping and surviving. Perhaps only the insider can know that he is not just "being there," but is on his way toward a promise.
- Walter Brueggemann

Without something greater than ourselves to ground our existence, our fragmented lives easily become like a grand old house on a poor foundation. No matter how good we are at covering the cracks, something fundamental is missing.
- Jonathan Wilson-Hartgrove

My wife and I have both experienced the disorientation of immigration. Years ago, God called my wife to move from Canada to go to school in the United States. Later, God called our family to move to Canada to serve in a local church. The bureaucratic challenges of moving from one country to another are complicated enough, but the culture shock is even more difficult. It can be difficult to know what things are called, where to go to get things fixed, or even what questions to ask. We were particularly surprised at the differences we discovered when moving between two closely related countries (the United States and Canada). It can be disconcerting to be at the bank or grocery store and suddenly realize that you are an outsider, an immigrant, that this place is not yet your home. Having moved to a foreign land, where is home?

After being cast out of Eden, the people of God ask, "Where is home?" In answer, God calls one man, Abram, and gives him a twofold promise: a child and a land. Both promises were partially fulfilled in the days of Abram and his descendants, but both promises waited for their true fulfillment in Jesus Christ. Our true home is in Jesus Christ. He is both the promised child and the promised land.

In order to hear the promise of land as the answer to our longings for home, we need to see how these two promises — of children and land — are tied together, how they are fulfilled in Christ, and then learn how to live as people still waiting on the final fulfillment of these promises.

LIVING OUTSIDE THE GARDEN

In the beginning, God created the heavens and the earth. God formed the world and filled it with life. He created man and woman in his image and gave them the responsibility to fill up, to care for, and to develop his creation.

Yet, Adam and Eve, our first parents, betray God and, in doing so, desecrate the land itself, bringing a curse upon the ground, upon the womb, and upon human relationships. Their children continue this betrayal and pollution of the land, when Cain kills his brother Abel and Abel's blood cries out from the ground.

For all their sin, though, God does not abandon his people. He clothes Adam and Eve and promises a child of Eve who will one day crush the serpent and end the enmity between God and us, between us and creation, and between all human beings (Gen 3:15). Yet violence, oppression, and wickedness continue to multiply until the "the thoughts of the human heart were only evil all the time" (Gen 6:5). So God cleanses the land with a mighty flood, saving only Noah and his family. Upon exiting the ark, Noah builds an altar to the LORD. Building the altar is an act of praise and a proclamation that this land belongs to the LORD. The LORD is King.

Yet, sin still taints the heart of Noah, who uses the fruit of the land to bring down more curses — getting drunk on wine, lying naked in his tent, and then cursing his grandson, Canaan. Having cleansed the earth and, in effect, started over, God reissues the call to fill the earth and rule over it, but the people do not listen. They gather on the plains of Shinar in order to make a name for themselves. They try to build a tower to heaven, but God comes down, confuses their languages and scatters them. The place is named Babel, which sounds like the Hebrew word for 'confused.'

After God's judgment at Babel, does God give up his project to redeem this world? No. However, instead of bringing another flood or issuing another command to the four corners of creation, God picks one man — Abram. As Walter Brueggemann points out, in the call of Abram, God "seizes people out of the history of expulsion and initiates them into the history of anticipation."[1] God's people are no longer outcasts from the Garden, but people on the way to the land of promise. However, the journey to the promise often moves through barren land.

HOLDING TO THE PROMISE

Abram is an unlikely choice. First, Abram is from the land of Babel. He was born in Ur of the Chaldeans — modern day

Iraq, ancient Babylon (Gen 11:31). Babylon's name is intimately connected with Babel, where the people gathered to make a name for themselves with a tower that reached to the heavens.

Furthermore, Abram is a pagan. While his father was still living, Abram's family left Ur and moved to Harran, but they did not leave their gods behind. Later, Joshua tells the Israelites when they gather at Shechem, "Long ago your ancestors — Terah and his sons Abraham and Nahor — lived beyond the Euphrates and served other gods" (Josh 24:2). Up to this point, Abram has not been a worshipper of the one true God, but has likely worshipped any number of gods from his home country, people, and father's household.

Lastly, Abram is an unlikely choice because he is an old, childless man. He has a nephew, Lot, but no children. His wife, Sarai, is barren (Gen 11:30) and Abram is seventy-five years old (Gen 12:4) — an unlikely choice to receive God's promise.

Yet repeatedly God promises Abram and Sarai both offspring and possession of land. For years they are forced to live trusting God's promises, yearning but not yet seeing fulfillment. Both the land and the people experience barrenness. An old man with a wife beyond the age of childbearing, Abram must trust in the goodness and power of God to do what he cannot imagine, bring forth a child from Sarai. A landless immigrant, Abram must trust in God to give him a place, a home.

Abram and Sarai spend years hearing these promises and seeing no progress. After Abram and his nephew Lot grow to have herds too large for the land to support, they are forced to part. Lot chooses the land that looks "like the garden of the Lord, like the land of Egypt" (Gen 13:10), but he ends up trapped in Sodom and Gomorrah. Abram lives in the land of Canaan and receives a promise from God: "Look around you from where you are, to the north and south, to the east and west. All the land that you see I will give to you and your offspring forever. I will make your offspring like the dust of the earth, so that if anyone were to count them, then your offspring could be counted. Go, walk through the length and breadth of the land, for I am giving it to you" (Gen 13:14-17). The promise of land and children are tied together, but there is still no progress. Abram and Sarai must continue to trust the promise, not what they see with their eyes or hold in their hands.

God promises Abram land and offspring, but Abram is forced to wait. He is promised land as far as his eye can see, but it is occupied and experiencing famine. He is promised children as numerous as the dust of the earth, but so far remains childless. His life is dry and barren. Even after God grants Abram a great victory that allows him to rescue his nephew Lot, we sense some exasperation in Abram as God comes with yet another promise:

> After this, the Word of the LORD came to Abram in a vision:
> "Do not be afraid, Abram.
> I am your shield,
> your very great reward."
> But Abram said, "Sovereign LORD, what can you give me since I remain childless and the one who will inherit my estate is Eliezer of Damascus?...You have given me no children so a servant in my household will be my heir. (Gen 15:1-3)

What can you give me, LORD? My future is dry and withered. No matter how much land you give or how often you protect me, I still remain without a child of my own. Abram trusts God and leaves home, country, and family.

Abram trusts God and places his entire future in God's hands. But will God keep his promises? Can God be trusted?

The LORD responds by giving another promise — numerous descendants for Abram, his own flesh and blood. He even shows Abram the stars in a vision to communicate the vast number of children that will come from his family. Abram believes God. God then promises land, but one question remains:

> Sovereign LORD, how can I know that I will take possession of it? (Gen 15:8)

Can God be trusted? Abram places what is most precious — his life and his future — into the hands of the LORD. The LORD responds by making a covenant with Abram, sealing their relationship with the blood of animals spilled, and with God himself walking between the pieces of the slain animals, vowing to keep his promises.

The LORD promises, but Abram and Sarai remain childless. Though they live in the land of Canaan, it is not theirs. They wander, leaning on the promise, moving in and out of the land they have been promised, but never settling there.

Sarai finally has enough. For ten years now, she has waited. Womb empty, home empty. Waiting until long past her childbearing years, but still empty. Her desire for a child and God's promise to Abram are in alignment, yet God seems inactive. The LORD spoke, the LORD promised, the LORD covenanted with Abram to give a child, but no child is found. Her womb remains empty. That emptiness aches.

> Now Sarai, Abram's wife, had borne him no children. But she had an Egyptian slave named Hagar, so she said to Abram, "The LORD has kept me from having children. Go,

sleep with my slave; perhaps I can build a family through her." (Gen 16:1-2)

The LORD has delayed and delayed, so Sarai takes the promise into her own hands. It is not an act of callousness, but one of anguished desperation. She hopes to accomplish the promise with her own resources. She takes initiative when the LORD seems silent and seeks to find a way around the barrier of her own barren body.

While Abram's union with Hagar brings forth Ishmael, it also gives birth to animosity between Sarai and Hagar. Sarai mistreats her and Hagar flees, only to meet an angel of the LORD who has heard her cry.

When Abram is ninety-nine, a full twenty-four years after he and Sarai first heard the promise of full womb and full land, the LORD appears to him again. He gives Abram and Sarai new names, signaling a new identity for both of them. The LORD again promises them children and land, but is now more specific. Abraham is promised the land of Canaan and Sarah is promised that she will bear Abraham a son, who will be called Isaac. The covenant is sealed by the sign of circumcision, which marks Abraham and his descendants as members of this covenant, as being the people of God.

Though Sarah laughs when she first hears the promise, it finally comes true. One year later, she holds a son, Isaac, in her arms. After decades, as Abraham and Sarah waited, God has kept his word. God has promised people and place, children and land, and now, at last, there is a beginning of the fulfillment of that promise.

LOOKING BEYOND THE LAND

In retracing Abraham and Sarah's history, we often focus on their struggle for a child. This elderly couple was barren and lived by the promise of God. This was true. However, this elderly couple was also landless, journeying far from home. As Alastair Roberts and Andrew Wilson note, they left without knowing the destination, trusting only God's call. "Abram, like Moses and Joshua, does not chart his own course, but has to trust that the Lord will lead him ("the land I will show you")."[2] They had to trust God's promise of the land as much as his promise of the child.

Abraham and Sarah could no more root themselves in a promised land than they could make Sarah's aged womb be filled with the promised child. For both land and children, God had to do for them what they could not do for themselves. "[Abraham's] family, which we later discover is large and prosperous, is being led from a land of barrenness into a Land of Promise, together with all their flocks and herds. This is an exodus journey in the making."[3] The land of promise is just as central a theme in the story as the child of promise. Both must be received by faith. As the book of Hebrews says of the whole family of Abraham, Isaac, and Jacob:

> All these people were still living by faith when they died. They did not receive the things promised; they only saw them and welcomed them from a distance, admitting that they were foreigners and strangers on earth. People who say such things show that they are looking for a country of their own. If they had been thinking of the country they had left, they would have had opportunity to return. Instead, they were longing for a better country—a heavenly one. Therefore God is not ashamed to be called their God, for he has prepared a city for them. (Heb 11:13-16).

Abraham, Sarah, and all their descendants lived and died waiting for the promise. They saw it only from a distance. They spent decades living in and around the land of Canaan, the land God would give their descendants. Yet they did not possess the land. Even as they walked on it, they welcomed it from a distance, because the land pointed beyond itself to something greater. The promise of the land points our hearts to our final promised home.

The land itself is not the goal — Jesus is. When we plant a garden, walk the streets of our neighborhood, and commit to a place for the long haul, we can be doing something good and right. God didn't make us to live nowhere, but somewhere. Just as Adam and Eve were set down in the garden of Eden, we have been set down in our place. We are embodied creatures who must and should live within the limits of place.

This is good, but this is not the goal. The promise of the land points farther than the land itself. Abraham and Sarah walk the land of Canaan, but they long for a better country. This longing is not an escape from the responsibilities, pains, or even the earthiness of human existence. This longing is a recognition that what transforms physical space into holy place, what turns Creation as a house into our true home, is the presence and work of God. The new heavens and new earth are glorious because there the dwelling place of God is among humanity (Rev 21:3). It is not the land itself, but the land as the place where the people of God live in the presence of God that is the goal.

Going local is good. Loving your place is good. Work the fields. Mend the fences. Love your people. Be where you are. It is easy and dangerous in our contemporary world to live disconnected from where we are, to live as if we are everywhere and nowhere. Yet, truly loving our place means looking beyond the romantic visions of organic gardens and neighborhood barbecues to find a greater vision.

Living rooted means recognizing that the land in which we live is not the land of promise. It means recovering a God-centered hope, where our true home is in Christ. This frees

our homes, neighborhoods, and cities to be what they are —
places where God is at work, where he is calling us to serve,
where he is shaping us for mission. Even when we move from
the exile from Eden and begin to walk in the land of Canaan,
we still long for a better country. No matter how good our
current homes are, they are not our true home. We are still
made for something greater, still called to something higher,
still longing for home.

Both promises — land and children — are fulfilled in
Jesus Christ. The promise of the child connects back with the
redemption promised in Genesis 3 — a child of Eve would be
born who would be struck by the serpent, but would crush his
head (Gen 3:15). The rest of the Old Testament can be seen,
in part, as the waiting, hoping, and searching for this promised
child, the one born to save. "She will give birth to a son, and
you are to give him the name Jesus, because he will save his
people from their sins." (Mt 1:21).

The promise of land connects with the original intent of
Eden. Though cast out of Eden, Abraham still receives God's
promise that his descendants will receive a place. In this place,
they will know *who* they were because they know *where* they
are. In this place, they will know life from and in the presence
of God and will live as grateful creatures made in God's image.
This land, like Eden before it, will be the beachhead of God's
mission in the world, now not only leading all creation in
praise of the Lord, but proclaiming God's salvation and
kingdom to a world under the power of sin. Most crucially, in
this land, God will be their God. "The whole land of Canaan,
where you now reside as a foreigner, I will give as an everlasting
possession to you and your descendants after you; and I will be
their God." (Gen 17:8). In Canaan, the people of God will live
in the presence of God. The land is where the people will find
their true rest and home in God.

Like Abraham, we are not merely exiled wanderers, but

people of the promise. God acts and works and moves. It is his work that will bring these promises to fulfillment. This humbles all our efforts to bring heaven to earth or to make this space into place. The work we do to root ourselves can only, at best, be a preparing of the soil, a pulling of weeds, a watering of the garden. We cannot make it grow. We cannot root ourselves, but must be rooted by God. We live as people of the promise.

THE PEOPLE OF PROMISE

The same pattern that we see in the life of Abraham continues in the life of his descendants. There is the promise of land, as well as the promise of children. God echoes these promises to Isaac, then to Jacob (Gen 28, 35), and then to all the sons of Jacob (Gen 48-49), who share in this promise of the land together. The struggle for children (and between children) continues. In particular, the covenant people struggle more deeply and wait longer for children. Abraham is promised as many children as the stars in the sky, but struggles to have any at all, while his brother Nahor has twelve (Gen 22:20-24). Isaac and Rebekah struggle twenty years to have Jacob and Esau, while Ishmael has twelve sons. These twelve sons become entire tribes, twelve princes from the family of Ishmael (Gen 25:13-18). Esau gives up his birthright, yet his family grows and grows (Gen 36). Jacob suffers under Laban, but eventually has twelve children of his own, though his family struggles with barrenness and death as well. The struggle for and with children continues as the sons of Jacob fail, one after the other, to live faithfully and even throw Joseph into a pit in the ground and later into the pit of slavery.

Yet, God continually promises to give them children. Though they wait and ache, God fulfills his promise. Abraham dies without land, but with an heir, Isaac. Isaac dies without land, but with an heir, Jacob. The promise is not completely fulfilled, but it is kept. Jacob dies outside of the land of Canaan, but with twelve sons. His last wish is that when he dies, his sons will bring his body and bury him in the land of promise.

The promise of children is kept, but the people still wait for the promise of the land. They still long for place. The full promise waits for the future. For now, they hold on in hope and trust.

They wait for the land. Generations live with the land as something they never see, but only receive as a promise from God. "Then the LORD said to him, "Know for certain that for four hundred years your descendants will be strangers in a country not their own and that they will be enslaved and mistreated there. But I will punish the nation they serve as slaves, and afterward they will come out with great possessions." (Gen 15:13-14). Land, for them, is a promise, not a possession.

Even when the patriarchs wander the land, it is not their own. It is something that comes to them only through the promise. Walter Brueggemann describes Israel as a people "on the way." "Israel is a landless people as we meet it earliest and most often in biblical faith. Although it is without place, it has a sense of being on the way to a promised place."[4]

We, like Israel, spend much of life without place, but on the way to a promised place. We live longing for roots, longing for a place where we belong. We get tastes of that promise here and now. We will find places, people, and practices (particularly in the church) that help root us where we are and shape us for mission and service. But we are always people on the way to the promised place. We are people on the way home. God walks beside us on the journey and will stand at the door welcoming us home.

Becoming rooted means paying special attention to our

land and our place. But it also means that our physical spaces, our homes, our neighborhoods, our cities, and our fields cannot fulfill the true desires of our hearts. They are good. We must care for them. God calls us to serve *these* people in *these* places. However, to confuse these places with the true land for which our heart longs, with the home for which we are made, puts more weight on them than they can bear. This is true even of the physical land of Israel, which is good and valuable, but is not the hope of the people of God.

Our longing for place finds its fulfillment in Christ. He is where we truly belong. The opening question of the Heidelberg Catechism asks, "What is your only comfort — in life and in death?" The answer — "That I am not my own, but belong — body and soul, in life and in death — to my faithful Savior Jesus Christ."[5] Jesus Christ is where we belong. He is where we find our life and where we find the stability that shapes us for mission and service. Ultimately, Jesus Christ is where our *place* is found.

Where is home? When the ground seems to shake beneath our feet and we cannot keep our footing, where is home? When we are suddenly reminded of how *this* place — this house or neighborhood — is not truly home, not where we truly belong, where is home?

God's people lived for centuries waiting to enter the promised land. They ached and groaned, longing for the promised child in the midst of barren wombs, longing for the promised land as they travelled in a barren land. They did not live as people who possessed the final ends of the promise, but had to live as people "on the way." They lived trusting God to keep his word. Eventually, they did receive children. Eventually, they did enter the promised land. God kept his promises, but the land was always meant to point to something beyond itself. It pointed to Jesus, our true home.

We, too, live as people "on the way." We, like Abraham and Sarah, know what it is like to live dry and withered. We have gone weeks, months, or years experiencing emptiness and waiting for the Lord to answer. Like Abraham and Sarah, many of us have followed the Lord when he did not reveal the destination, when he did not tell us more than the next faithful step. And, like Abraham and Sarah, living outside the land, waiting for the return of Jesus, we fix our eyes on the future kingdom even as we live in the present. While we should seek to grow more rooted in our local place, the hope of the patriarchs (and the hope of scripture) is not the land itself, but Jesus Christ. In him, we find our true home, which enables us to work more deeply for the good of our earthly homes.

Though the land pointed ahead to Christ, it was also a place where God shaped his people to live as *his* people, people shaped by the presence and promises of God.

3

LOVE WHERE YOU ARE

THE PURPOSE OF LIFE IN THE LAND

*Our hunger for "community" may be the clearest contempo-
rary expression of the heart's yearning for its true home.*
  - Jonathan Wilson-Hartgrove

We find ourselves in community; we need friends on the road.
  - James K. A. Smith

W hat do you do when you finally get there? I felt
oddly let down after purchasing our first home.
I was so excited for a place that would be *ours*. A
house where we could invest our sweat and energy, trans-
forming it into a home. A house that would become *our* place.
House-hunting was a whirlwind and I love the house we
purchased, but once we moved in, the magic began to wear
off. I noticed where the previous paint job was not quite right.
The dishwasher started making funny noises. I discovered that
the corner of the back deck was sinking a little. The perfect
pictures and perfect walk-through came crashing down into
the reality of an imperfect house. My perfect dream lasted only

until I actually moved in. Then, I had to learn to love the house I had, not the one I had pictured in my mind.

Living rooted means learning to love where you are, not where you wish you were. When God's people finally entered the land of Israel, they were placed in family plots alongside neighbors. There, they learned to love God and neighbor, learned to live as God's people. The community and stability of life in the land made it possible for them to grow in love.

Though we live outside the land of Israel, our homes, churches, and neighborhoods are arenas where we grow in love of God and neighbor. Instead of searching for an ideal place to live out our faith, we must live with and for Jesus in the messy reality of everyday life.

ENTERING THE LAND

After four hundred years in Egypt and forty years in the wilderness, God's people enter the promised land. At long last, they have a place to call home. As God promised, "The LORD your God will give you rest by giving you this land" (Josh 1:13). Entering the land is a foretaste of entering into God's rest.

The land is a gift from God. When years earlier, Moses sent twelve spies to look in on the land, they came back reporting that the land was inhabited by giants. All but two of the spies advised against entering the land. For them, it was a scary place full of people far too strong for them (Num 13:28). At that time, God's people were afraid. They compared their strength to the strength of those already living in the land and chose not to enter the promised land.

Joshua, like Moses before him, sends spies into the land, who bring back a very different report. "The LORD has surely given the whole land into our hands; all the people are melting in fear because of us" (Josh 2:24). Instead of trembling in fear at the power of the people of the land, Joshua's spies encourage confidence in God and his promises. This time, they trust God and enter the land. God's presence, symbolized in the Ark of the Covenant, goes ahead of them into the waters of the Jordan River, carried by the priests. Just as the Red Sea parted when God brought Israel out of Egypt, the Jordan divides when God brings them into the land (Josh 3). Both times, though, the people cross on dry ground.

The Lord brings them into the land. It is not their strength, military skills, or holiness that earn them the land. God makes it possible. The people of God are far from perfect and the road is far from easy. They encounter resistance and fight battles. They fail and need to repent. They compromise when they should not. But in spite of it all, God gives the land into their hands. Along with the land, God gives them rest. "The LORD gave them rest on every side, just as he had sworn to their ancestors. Not one of their enemies withstood them; the LORD gave all their enemies into their hands. Not one of all the LORD's good promises to Israel failed; every one was fulfilled" (Josh 21:44-45).

Having entered the land, the people now enter rest. They have peace, the rest of finally coming home, even if it is a home none of them has ever seen before.

BOUNDARY LINES

When God's people enter Canaan, the land is divided between the twelve tribes. While all the land ultimately belongs to the LORD ("The land must not be sold permanently, because the land is mine and you reside in my land as foreigners and strangers" Lev 25:23), God gives portions of the land to each of the tribes of Israel. The Levites are given cities instead of their own territory, but the rest of the land is divided among the tribes. The lot is cast and God's will is revealed as to where each tribe and family will be located.

The book of Joshua spends eight whole chapters detailing which land and which cities belong to which tribes (Josh 13-21). As Joshua tells us, the tribes do not get to pick their land. They do not swap prime real estate based upon their preferences and choices. They cannot choose a larger or smaller portion. Instead, they receive the land from the hand of God. Their place in the land is not a result of their effort, but is instead a gift from God. No tribe needs to wonder where they belong. Instead, they can rest knowing they are right where God wants them to be.

In addition to dividing the land among the tribes, the tribes are tasked with dividing up their territories into family parcels of land. Each family receives a plot that is their ancestral inheritance (Num 13:23, 36:5-11; 1 Kgs 21:3). This plot is that family's special piece of the land of Israel. It is *their* place. It is not determined by how rich or poor, strong or weak, righteous or unrighteous the family is. They each receive a place, a plot of land.

These plots of land are divided by boundary lines. Over the course of generations, farmers had picked stones out of the fields as part of preparing the soil. These stones had been stacked along the boundaries of the field, forming a natural stone fence line. These boundary lines serve to divide the various family plots. Each family receives a plot and a place that is theirs as a gift from the LORD. Thus, David can say, "The boundary lines have fallen for me in pleasant places; surely I have a delightful inheritance." (Ps 16:6). David delights in the plot God gave him.

These boundary lines are meant to be permanent. In Deuteronomy 27, prior to entering the land itself, the people receive instructions from God, telling them to gather upon two mountains once they cross the Jordan. Once there, they are to proclaim God's commands, with the people responding by saying 'Amen.'

In the midst of commands against sexual sins, against withholding justice from foreigners, and against leading the blind astray is a command regarding boundary lines: ""Cursed is anyone who moves their neighbor's boundary stone." Then all the people shall say, "Amen!""" (Deut 27:17). Some enterprising or wicked Israelite may have been tempted to enlarge his family's holdings by moving the boundary stones. Yet, the LORD calls this action cursed. God's people are not to gain more by taking from others. The place they have been given is enough for them. Taking more by moving the boundary stone shows a lack of trust in God and a lack of love for the neighbor whose land they have stolen.

Though the boundary stones cannot be moved, the land can be sold. This was part of the drama of Ahab and Naboth (1 Kgs 21). King Ahab wanted Naboth's inherited land, but Naboth refused to sell the land because it was given to him by the LORD and handed down by his fathers. Ahab and his wife, Jezebel, circumvented Naboth's resistance by having Naboth falsely denounced and killed. In doing so, Ahab worked not only to take Naboth's life, but also to take his family's place within the land of Israel. The prophet Elijah then pronounced severe judgment upon Ahab and Jezebel, and upon their entire household for this action.

Though the land can be sold, it cannot be sold permanently. If poverty forces someone to sell some portion of their inherited land, it can always be bought back. According to Leviticus 25:13-28, the seller's nearest relative must step in and buy back land that has been sold. If the seller can get enough money to buy back the land, he will always have that opportunity.[1]

We see this playing out in the book of Ruth. Boaz's negotiation with the kinsman at the city gates is about Ruth and

Naomi's protection and place within the family, but it is also about the physical place — land, inheritance — that must be bought back for this family. Redemption for Naomi and Ruth is restoration of both people and place.

However, even if the seller or a close family member cannot get the money to buy back the land, the land will only go to the buyer until the time of Jubilee. In Israel, every fiftieth year (after the seventh set of seven years) is known as a Jubilee, a year of restoration in Israel. Slaves are set free, debts are cancelled, and land that has been sold reverts back to the original families (Lev 25). Jubilee is freedom and cancellation of debts, but it is also a restoration of place. This plot, this place, is yours. It is a gift from God to you. Even if you sell it or lose it, it will eventually be restored to you.

As a picture of salvation, Jubilee points to God's gifts of freedom from the bondage of sin and of wiping away of our debts before him. Yet, it also points to salvation as the restoration of our place in God's house, our place in the land that God gave us. Salvation is freedom and forgiveness and coming home.

After leading the people out of Egypt and walking with them for forty years in the wilderness, God brings them into the land he promised. He divides the land for each tribe and then for each family. He gives each family a plot and tells the families that the shape and size of their plots shall not change. When the plot sold, it should be bought back. Even when that is not possible, the land will still eventually be restored at the Jubilee. Those brought into the land will never permanently lose their place in it.

Why was this so important?

The land is a school where Israel learns to live as God's people. Like Eden, the land of Israel is a place, not simply space. God's people have been set down in a specific plot of land and called to grow roots there. Like Eden, Israel is meant to be a beachhead of God's kingdom mission. God places them in this land, but with a mission as wide as the world.

Yet, to live out that mission, they need to learn to live as God's people. They need to learn God's ways — to love God and love neighbor. God has spent forty years with them in the wilderness, teaching them his will and his ways, laying down his good Law for them. They are to live it out so that the world will know God and come to worship him. God brings them into the land of Israel, gives them a plot of land and says, in essence, "Here. This is where you live out my will in the world. The goal is the ends of the earth, but you are called to start here, to do it here first." God roots them in the land to serve this greater purpose of growing them in love of God and neighbor, for the sake of God's kingdom mission in the world.

COMMUNITY

God also roots his people in community. He sets them down as a nation in the midst of other peoples, people who have rubbed against them at their borders and have even struggled with them as they came into the land. God also sets down each tribe and family right next to each other. Even the design of the homes in ancient Israel was intended so that families and tribes could live together.[2] The people of God are not hermits living out in the desert, but people and families living together in community. This is how they are to live out God's will in the world — together.

Most of God's commands assume we live in community with other people. If faithfulness were simply about avoiding sin, wrongdoing, or temptation, we might understand the desire to withdraw to a quiet place where we could put all our effort into sin-avoidance. Yet, as many Christians can attest throughout the ages, going off by ourselves is not an avenue to righteousness. We cannot run from ourselves, and the devil pursues us. Even if it were possible to avoid lust and greed and idolatry by avoiding people, living God's will is not just about avoiding doing wrong, but about living *for* God. We cannot love our neighbor when we live away from all other people. We cannot care for the widow, the orphan, and the alien when we keep ourselves from them. Living as God's people requires community.

Living rooted is not done in isolation, but with others. Even those called to move from the world into monastic communities do so *in* communities. The solitary monk is rare and often dangerous. As Jonathan Wilson-Hartgrove says, "The trouble, all the saints insist, is that we cannot find stability within ourselves alone."[3] We are made to live out God's will together. As Saint Augustine said in his monastic rule: "Whenever you go out, walk together, and when you reach your destination, stay together."[4] We live for God together in community.

You likely do not live in the promised land of Israel. You probably do not have a small family plot that has been passed down for generations and was originally given to your family by God himself. However, God has placed you where you are. Your home, your community, your neighborhood are not yours by accident. It is there that God calls you to live your life for him. This is where God calls you to be rooted so you can live his will.

However, in modern life, we frequently self-select our communities. Community is often divorced from geography. We join groups based upon shared interests, not shared space. We may feel closer to people in another country — people who like the same books we do, for example — than to the neighbor across the street.

Shared interests are good and beneficial for friendship, but there is danger in choosing our communities. If we choose to join, we can choose to leave. If my book group hates this book

I love, I can leave the group and never come back. If the people in the chat room challenge my opinions on foreign policy, I can simply block them or leave the chat. With the click of a button, we can join a new community. But with the same click of a button, we can also unfriend, unsubscribe, or unfollow.

When we always choose who is in our "community," all relationships become fragile. I grew up hearing "you can pick your friends, but you cannot pick your relatives." Family was seen as the one community that was a given, that you were stuck with forever and that you had to learn to love no matter what.

However, we see even family coming under the pressure of self-selected communities. We hear people talk about how their true family are their friends. We hear people say, "if your parents don't support you, I will be your mom/dad" or "if your family doesn't agree with you, they are not your true family." There can be deep pain and trauma within families, but people do not cease to be our family because they are difficult. Everywhere we look, even in television shows, the big moments of life (weddings, funerals, births) are now populated by coworkers, instead of family members.

Living rooted means sticking with people and letting people stick with us. It means forming deeper and more lasting communities. "My well-being is tied up with the health of my neighbor — even my enemy — and the place on earth that we share."[5] Christians should be people who actually know their neighbors and who are committed in their friendships. We cannot live this life of faith alone.

Self-selecting community has also impacted the church. Before the advent of the automobile, people went to church where they lived. This was a matter of practical necessity. Once driving became possible, most people still worshipped where their families were. Yet, we now can choose to go somewhere other than the church closest to us. If we don't like the preaching, find the people too difficult, or are hurt in some way, we can go to the church across town or in another town altogether. The opportunities created by the ability to travel make church commitments more fragile.

Some churches respond with fear, telling their members they are the only true church and warning hellfire for those who have left. Many other churches feel the need to compete with each other, providing the best set of services for the religious consumer. But every church knows that any member, if they desire, can leave and go to a different church. Like it or not, this has changed how pastors preach and provide spiritual direction, and how churches minister as a whole.

While the whole community of Israel was rooted in the land, our communities will likely not be so stable. Particularly in the city, people frequently move jobs and homes. My own neighborhood has seen significant turnover in the last couple years as entire communities migrated because of increased opportunities for working from home. "Community is always a risk. We cannot know beforehand who will stay and who will leave. But each decision to stay — every prayer lifted up from our half-born condition — can be seen as an act of faith that our God will give us what we need."[6] Community is a risk, but a risk worth taking, because it is only here that we can learn to live as God's people.

Community is the place God gives us to live our calling. It is also where we discern our calling. We cannot even find ourselves by ourselves. We need friends. "The friend who leaps ahead is one who's glimpsed what you're called to be and is willing to let you be uncomfortable as you wrestle with the call, who loves you enough to let you struggle for your soul but is standing by with a bandage and a map."[7] We need friends, family, neighbors, and — above all — brothers and sisters in Christ to love in order to live God's calling in our lives. But we also need friends, family, neighbors, and — above all — brothers and sisters in Christ to love *us* if we are to know our true calling in Jesus Christ.

STABILITY AND LOVE OF NEIGHBOR

Being rooted in the land also provides stability. Learning to love God and neighbor takes time in the same place. One of the greatest dangers of our current cultural rootlessness is inability to sit still long enough to learn to love. By constantly moving (literally or otherwise), we stunt our ability to grow in love.

Love of neighbor requires a place. It requires flesh and blood people near us and the time to know and love them well. Jonathan Wilson-Hartgrove laments learning this lesson the hard way, "I wanted to love my neighbor, but I had not stayed in one place long enough to know my neighbors or my neighborhood."[8] The deeper the love, the closer we often need to be to one another. That closeness does not develop overnight. It can take time for people to let us into their lives (and for us to do the same). Small acts of love, like bringing in the garbage bins or holding onto packages while we are on vacation, can be done between neighbors with little risk or commitment. If one neighbor moves out and another moves in, we can engage in the same acts of neighborly kindness. The particular neighbor — their story, their struggles, their passions — has little to do with these acts of neighborliness.

Yet to move beyond neighborly kindness into genuine love for our neighbors requires time and space for relationship and vulnerability to develop. We cannot do this if we are always moving. The people of God were placed in the land and rooted in specific plots with specific neighbors. They were placed in this stable community in order to learn how to love their God and love one another. The permanence of the plots was part of the point. The people were given a place and neighbors to love and be loved by.

As a pastor, I have the privilege to walk with people during some of the most difficult seasons of their lives. I am called to listen, pray, and occasionally speak when people walk through the deep valleys and seek to walk those valleys with Jesus. Yet, like most pastors, I find that it takes time to be allowed into those moments. In the first few months or years you spend in a community, you will only have certain people who will let you know their struggles. Often, their crisis is so large they cannot hold it back, the family is so desperate they are willing to bring in the new pastor, or they simply have a deep level of institutional trust in the pastoral office.

At this point, I am often let in because of my office, not because of our relationship. However, as the months and years pass and I spend more and more time with these people — more cups of coffee, more casual conversations, more time preaching and listening and loving as best I can — something changes. It does not happen overnight. It develops at different speeds with different people. Slowly, though, I am welcomed into those places that need to hear of the love and care of Jesus. When I am, it is a holy thing.

Most pastors I talk to think it takes about seven years in a congregation before this happens. Seven years!

It can take years for people to share their struggles with their own pastor, but it is part of the pastor's particular calling to foster and facilitate this. This is not a complaint, but a recognition of the time needed to develop relationships where love can grow well.

If it is true for pastors, then it is also true for life in our neighborhoods. Loving our neighbors takes time. We need to know each other for love to grow beyond the bounds of neighborliness. In the short term we can be kind. We can be nice. We can be good and decent and helpful to one another. All this is good. But the cost of doing those things is minimal — socially, financially, and even spiritually. The costly love — the costly discipleship that we are called to as God's people — requires relationship. The risk of genuine love — love in the way of Jesus — requires real relationship with our neighbors. This cannot be done overnight. "The most important thing most of us can do to grow spiritually is to stay in the place where we are."[9]

These relationships do not develop automatically. We need time, of course, but time itself is not enough. We can live in the same place for decades, but instead of spending time reaching out in love, we can spend it building walls to protect ourselves, keeping others from seeing our neediness or us from seeing their brokenness.[10] Twenty years on the same street, but we might not know the names of people who live two doors down. We may know their names, but we have never said more than a passing word or two to them. We may have never known each other enough to let them in on our struggles.

Sometimes neighborhoods themselves develop as a way of protecting ourselves, of keeping ourselves from experiencing or being exposed to the brokenness. We've seen zoning regulations, intended to 'improve the community,' used instead as a way of driving out the poor and the undesirables. We do not always have to move our house to get rid of our neighbors. We can sometimes stay in one place and grow less loving, instead of more.

God gives his people land and neighbors to love. In placing the people in the land, God is telling them, "This is your place and these are your neighbors — forever. These are the people you will have to learn to love. If you are going to learn to live as my people and love your neighbors, it is going to be *here*, with *these* people."

There are still communities where people have lived in the same neighborhood for decades. However, this is growing more and more rare. In a world of rapid mobility, we often leave our communities, our churches, our work, and even our friendships before they have the opportunity to blossom into genuine love. "In short, stability's wisdom insists that spiritual growth depends on human beings rooting ourselves in a place on earth with other creatures."[11] Stability is God's gift so his people can learn to love their neighbor.

We do not know how long we are called to be in one place. There can be good and genuine reasons to move to new neighborhoods, change jobs, and even (on rare occasions) change churches. Yet, for the time God has given us in a place, we must give ourselves to that community in order to be able to love God and our neighbor well. "Whether we think we have options or not, the wisdom of stability suggests that we can only begin to grow spiritually by accepting the gift of faith in the place where we are."[12] Just as Israel was given the soil of community as the field where they were to cultivate love of God and neighbor, we have to love God and neighbor *here* if we are going to do it anywhere.

As much as stability will teach us to love our neighbor, it will also teach us to be loved by our neighbor. We have to learn to forgive, to serve, and to have compassion for our neighbor, even when they are difficult to love. It will not always be easy to get along with our neighbors. But, then, we are not always that easy to love, either. We can be cranky, distant, and difficult, too. Gregory the Great, when instructing pastors on how to care for the souls of married people in their charge gave this advice: "The married should be advised, then, that they not worry themselves so much about what they must endure from their spouse but consider what their spouse must endure on account of them. For if one really considers what must be endured on his account, it is all the easier to bear the things of others."[13] Consider not only what you have to bear in others, but what they must bear in you as well.

God gives Israel a place, a place where the boundary lines have fallen in pleasant places, so they can learn to live as his people. In this place and with these people, they learn to love God and neighbor according to God's ways. Their place is permanent, their land cannot be sold forever. They will always be called back to that land. Living in the West, however, many of us have the chance to move. We might not take that opportunity, but we all face the temptation to flee when love gets hard.

THE TEMPTATION TO FLEE TO TARSHISH

I once knew a family who seemed to move every couple of years. They would buy a beautiful house and spend much time and energy on it. Just when it was finally becoming home, the 'For Sale' sign would appear on the lawn. One or both of them had become bored and felt like they "needed a change of scenery." I always felt a powerful sense of loss for them, as I watched this pattern play out over and over again. Why did they keep moving houses when so many long for one home? Why put their kids through the challenges of growing up in six or seven different houses? Why did they leave just when things were finally settling?

As a culture, we can be tempted to look for something new when things get difficult — a different job, a different church, a different home. While there may be times when moving on is right, this often masks our restless spirit. People are often less exciting, more mundane, or even more ugly in real life. Disappointed with what we find, we can be tempted to move on. Relationships, homes, work, and church are all less glamorous in real life than in the photo-shopped images in our heads. Months in, the relationship doesn't have the same spark as it did on the first date, so we move on. We learn that the house that looked perfect when we bought it suddenly has chipped paint and nail holes everywhere and we grow discontented. We discover that the church we thought was *the* place where everything was finally going to be right turns out to be filled with sinners just like the last one. So we flee, looking for perfection, but landing only in perpetual immaturity.

Right when we need most to be rooted, to stay with our discomfort, and to listen well for what God is saying to us, we want to leave. We live on the surface instead of setting down and establishing roots. In doing so, we often miss opportunities for growth in Christian maturity. Perseverance is a pathway to maturity.

Pastor Eugene Peterson calls this impulse "fleeing to Tarshish." Drawing from the story of Jonah, Peterson says we are tempted to flee from the mundane work God has called us to in favor of the glamour of somewhere else. God calls us to Nineveh, but we flee to Tarshish.

> And why Tarshish? For one thing, it is a lot more exciting than Nineveh. Nineveh is an ancient site with layer after layer of ruined and unhappy history. Going to Nineveh to preach was not a coveted assignment for a Hebrew prophet with good references. But Tarshish was something else. Tarshish was exotic. Tarshish was adventure. Tarshish had the appeal of the unknown furnished with baroque details from the fantasizing imagination.[14]

But Tarshish is just a dream. Part of the beauty of Tarshish is that we don't know its exact location – it is just somewhere "over there." The Bible gives us hints, but we do not know precisely where to find it. It is as if we aren't supposed to really know where Jonah is going, only that his greatest desire is to go in the opposite direction from where God wants him to go.

Jonah wants to continue his ministry, to continue being a disciple, but on his own terms, and where he wants. "God, I'll serve you, but only if I get to pick where. Only in Tarshish. Some far-off place, but not where you want me. God, I'll do whatever you want, just don't send me to *those* people." Jonah's dream of what it means to be God's people, of who should be in and who should be out, is so important that he flees. He flees from the presence of the Lord.

By contrast, Nineveh is a well-known place. Nineveh is a growing power in the time of Jonah, but a power that prides itself on cruelty and the utter destruction of its enemies. Nineveh does not want just to defeat you, they want to break you. When they invade, their armies do not just take your food and lay siege to your cities — they chop down all your trees, burn your fields, and destroy your countryside. When they inevitably win, they separate and scatter the survivors to the four corners of their empire so that their cultural memory and shared identity will be crushed.

No one in their right mind would want to go to Nineveh. It is an ugly, brutal place. Yet, this is where Jonah is called. It's not the place he would have chosen, but it is the place where God has called him.

Most of our lives, our callings, our neighbors are more like Nineveh than Tarshish. Living as a Christian is often more like mucking out the barn in Nineveh than living in the air-brushed glamor of Tarshish. People are difficult. Conditions are hard. It is messy and dirty work trying to live with Jesus in *this* place with *these* people. We might imagine it would be easier somewhere else. We think the answer to our spiritual problems lies just beyond the horizon in Tarshish. If we can get to the right place and find the right conditions, then we will finally turn the corner and start coasting.

So we are tempted to flee somewhere else: literally, emotionally, and/or spiritually. Instead, of working in the Nineveh-like conditions in which we all find ourselves in, we look for relief elsewhere. To paraphrase Eugene Peterson,

"There is not an honest [Christian] in the land who is not deeply aware of the slum conditions that exist in the [Christian life] and, therefore, the unending task of clearing out the garbage, finding space for breathing, getting adequate nourishment, and venturing into the streets day after day, night after night, risking life and limb in acts of faith and love. We experience this week after week, year after year. Some weeks it is better, some weeks a little worse. But always it is there."[15]

Being rooted often means sticking it out in Nineveh, instead of fleeing to Tarshish. Again, there are sometimes good and genuine reasons to leave, but often our spiritual questing disguises a deep inner restlessness and immaturity. No matter how hard we run toward Tarshish, we cannot outrun ourselves and we certainly cannot outrun God. We are better off doing the hard, dirty work of dealing with our sin and brokenness, and of dealing with God and our neighbor. This is the pathway to learning to be God's people. If we leave or go searching as soon as love becomes difficult, we may end up, like Jonah, running from the presence of the Lord.

To paraphrase Peterson again, "The [Christian] must learn to live with his or her own darkness, with the interior horror or temptation and fantasy. Salvation affects the whole of the psyche; to try to escape boredom, sexual frustration, restlessness, unsatisfied desire by searching for fresh tasks and fresh ideas is to attempt to seal off these areas from grace. Without the humiliating and wholly "unspiritual" experiences of parish-life — the limited routine of trivial tasks, the sheer tedium and loneliness — there would be no way of confronting much of human nature. It is a discipline to destroy illusions."[16]

LOVE WHERE YOU ARE

God brought Israel into the land. God divided the land up among the tribes, giving sections to each family. He placed families side-by-side, giving them neighbors to love. He rooted Israel in the land so that they would learn how to be his people. Because love grows locally, God planted his people with families, neighbors, and friends. He gave them community. The system of family plots was designed, in part, to keep people from moving too quickly, so they could do the long, hard work of growing to love each other.

The temptation to get up and move when life or relationships become challenging is not new. However, it is easier than ever before. But a tree transplanted too often never develops roots. It never grows and bears fruit. God has planted us in neighborhoods, in families, and in communities as well. It is here we learn to love God and love our neighbor. We learn to live as God's people in the challenging and beautiful space of real relationships.

There are no perfect jobs. There are no perfect churches. There are no perfect families or neighborhoods or homes this side of Jesus' return. We can mask the wrinkles and warts with photoshop or Instagram filters, but they exist in every community, in every family, and in every church. "Practicing stability has meant unlearning the habits of a culture that tells us the answer to our problems is always somewhere else."[17] Love where you are. Love the family you have, not the one you wish you had. Love the church you have been given, not the one you wish you went to. Love the place where you have been rooted, not the imaginary neighborhood of your dreams. Learn to love and live with the Lord in Nineveh, and set aside searching for Tarshish.

4

LAND OF FORGETFULNESS

THE DANGER OF LIFE IN THE LAND

Gradually it dawned on me that the crevasse was not before me, but within me.

- Eugene Peterson

Part of the reason we can hold our beliefs so lightly is that what is truly important to us is not only or primarily our beliefs but how they affect our identity.

- Alan Noble

Finally, Israel enters the land. This land is a place for learning to love our neighbor, but it is also a place of spiritual danger. Place is a gift and a calling. The land itself is not all it was cracked up to be — it turns out we are longing for something the land itself cannot give. There are spiritual temptations upon entering the land, upon becoming rooted, that we do not face beforehand. We must recognize these dangers so that we do not expect too much from our place and forget God.

THE LAND AS SPIRITUAL TEMPTATION

Moses speaks the most haunting words in the whole Penta-teuch as the people sit at the edge of the promised land. The Lord, through Moses, gives astounding promises about the kind of land God is giving to them:

> Observe the commands of the Lord your God, walking obedience to him and revering him. For the Lord your God is bringing you into a good land — a land with brooks, streams, and deep springs gushing out in the valleys and hills; a land with wheat and barley, vines and fig trees, pome-granates, olive oil and honey; a land where bread will not be scarce and you will lack nothing; a land where the rocks are iron and you can dig copper out of the hills. (Deut 8:6-9)

This is a land of abundance. After four hundred years of eating the bread of slavery and death in Egypt, and another forty years in the wilderness, the people of God enter a good and fruitful land. We can almost imagine the joy and gratitude on the lips of the people. "Thank you, Lord! Finally we have a home. Finally we have stability. Finally we are safe. Finally we have *a place*, and all thanks to the goodness of our great God!" However much we might imagine thankfulness as the natural response to being finally brought into the land for which we have longed, God warns of a different outcome:

> When you have eaten and are satisfied, praise the Lord your God for the good land he has given you. Be careful that you do not forget the Lord your God, failing to observe his commands, his laws and his decrees that I am giving you this day. Otherwise, when you eat and are satisfied, when you build fine houses and settle down, and when your herds

and flocks grow large and your silver and gold increase and all you have is multiplied, then your heart will become proud and you will forget the LORD your God, who brought you out of Egypt, out of the land of slavery. He led you through the vast and dreadful wilderness, that thirsty and waterless land, with its venomous snakes and scorpions. He brought you water out of hard rock. He gave you manna to eat in the wilderness, something your ancestors had never known, to humble and test you so that in the end it might go well with you. You may say to yourself, "My power and the strength of my hands have produced this wealth for me." But remember the LORD your God, for it is he who gives you the ability to produce wealth, and so confirms his covenant, which he swore to your ancestors, as it is today (Deut 8:10-18).

Once they enter the land, instead of being thankful, they will grow forgetful. For forty years in the wilderness, the people grumbled, they rebelled, they pined for Egypt, but they did not forget God altogether. God sustained them every day by manna and quail. God made water pour forth from hard rock so they could drink. They lived with the constant reminder of God's provision. But now they come into the land, where rivers, brooks, and streams flow; where wheat, barley, and olives grow; where they have everything they need and more, and where they will forget God.

It is a haunting and damning passage. Entering the land is not the end of the struggle, but the beginning of a different one. God's blessings were meant to lead the people closer to God and into praise and gratitude. Instead, they lead to pride. As soon as the manna stops raining, they begin to think their blessings come from their own work.

God's people have longed for *a place* since being exiled from Eden. They have lived with the promise of home for generations. They have walked with God on the way toward the promise in the wilderness. Yet, when they are finally given this place, they manage to twist it. Instead of singing the doxology — "Praise God from whom all blessings flow" — they begin to sing a very different tune: "Praise *me* from whom all blessings flow."

Forgetfulness is the great sin of Israel in the land. As John Calvin attests, "Although God, by his benefits, gently allures us to himself, as it were by a taste of his fatherly sweetness, yet there is nothing into which we more easily fall than into a forgetfulness of him, when we are in the enjoyment of peace and comfort."[1] Blessing should lead to gratitude, but instead it often leads to forgetfulness. In pain and suffering, we cry out to God. We can hardly forget God in the painful heat of the wilderness (even if we fear his absence). However, when we are comfortable and the trials have passed, we quickly forget about God. We go back to our "normal life," which is life with God at the margins, if God is thought of at all.

This is true for Israel in the land. God and his will are ignored and the people become the center. God's solemn warning comes true as the people forget him again and again. The period of the judges is a repeated cycle: the people forget God, they fall into sin and bondage, they cry out for help, God raises up a judge who delivers the people, and then the judge leads them for a time. However, once the judge dies, the people quickly fall back into forgetfulness. It is a time "where everyone did what was right in his own eyes" (Judg 21:25 ESV).

Even after God anoints a king, this pattern of forgetfulness persists. The king turns into a Pharaoh-like figure who oppresses his people with forced labor (1 Kgs 5:13, 12:4). Solomon begins to forget God's ways towards the end of his life (1 Kgs 11:4). The kingdom divides after Solomon's death and the tribes slowly spiral toward destruction.

There are occasionally good kings in Judah, such as Hezekiah and Josiah, who seek the Lord, as David had. The Lord consistently sends prophets to call the people to remember him. The book of Kings reads like a tragedy, where the beloved people of God slowly decay, the bright spots overshadowed by darkness. The end is exile, with the people, who have forgotten their God, ripped from the very land God has given them. Yet, as we will see later, this is not the end. Just as there was a promise on the other side of Eden, there is a promise on the far side of exile. God will provide a true restoration, not only to physical place, but to our true home in God — but that is a story for another chapter.

As they stand on the brink of entering the land, the people are warned by the LORD not to forget him. Most of them ignore that warning. They have received the land *from* God, but they want the land *apart from* God. They use the gifts of God to escape from life with God. They want to enjoy the blessings of God without having to deal with God himself. They want all the security, the peace, and the provision of God without the risky and costly relationship with God.

Most dangerously, it does not seem as if the people actively choose this path. Some willfully walk away from God and consciously reject the word of the prophets, but most simply drift. In times of pain and suffering, they cry out to the LORD. Yet, as soon as deliverance comes and comfort envelopes them, they forget God again. They work in their shops or in their fields, sweating and straining, and begin to feel proud of themselves, rather than thankful to God.

In the Exodus, God's work was clear and easy to see. But in the daily grind of work and family, the Israelites can see *their* work and its results, and it grows easy to cut God out of the equation. "You may say to yourself, "My power and the strength of my hands have produced this wealth for me.""" (Deut 8:17). Comfort breeds forgetfulness.

All this happens when they are in the land. The land is good. The gift of place is still good. It is an immense blessing from God to find a place where we experience belonging and calling, where we can live our faith in the midst of brothers and sisters, neighbors, and enemies. Yet, it is not enough. Israel has all these blessings and more, but they need more than the land; they need the Lord.

Deuteronomy 8 is a haunting passage because it confronts us with the same warning given to Israel. Like the Israelites, do we forget God? When we can finally afford *the* house and we move in and find a place for everything and at long last give a deep sigh of contentment, do we also find ourselves drifting from God, our hearts and minds occupied with other things? When the storm was raging and everything seemed to be coming apart at the seams, we felt the Lord's presence as he held us together. We could do nothing and he held us in his arms. But now that the storm has passed, we might begin to think (even unconsciously), "God, now I can hold myself. Back then, I couldn't do it. Thank you. But now, life is calmer and more manageable. I can take it from here." Blessing, comfort, and peace leading people to forget God is not just the ancient story of Israel. It is so often our own story.

Deuteronomy 8 is also haunting because it confronts us with the inadequacy of the land itself. Being in the land did not protect Israel from the temptations that came with comfort, ease, and blessing. Likewise, being physically rooted in our communities and neighbors does not provide us with automatic resistance to the same temptations.

It is not enough to simply stay put, as good as that may be. It is not enough to have an acreage, raise some chickens, and plant a garden. It is not enough to simply set down roots in the soil of a location, if we do not have our roots in God first. It was not enough for Israel. They were rooted in the land, given a place, a community, and a context in which to live out their calling as God's people. Yet, they lost sight of where the blessings came from. They forgot who made the land produce and the rains fall, or who strengthened their hands for success. They forgot what Solomon once sang:

> Unless the Lord builds the house,
>   the builders labor in vain.
> Unless the Lord watches over the city,
>   the guards stand watch in vain.
> In vain you rise early
>   and stay up late,
> toiling for food to eat—
>   for he grants sleep to those he loves. (Ps 127:1-2).

AVOIDING AND FORGETTING GOD

Like Israel before us, we can seek to enjoy God's blessings without having to deal with God himself. As it was for Israel before us, this can at times be a conscious decision, but it can also sneak up on us. Even when we feel rooted in the land, we can experience rootlessness as we find ourselves forgetting God.

The Quest for Security: Tucked into the longing for place and rootedness is a desire for security. For a house to be a home, for a space to become a place, it must be safe. But where do we find security? Many of us grow up hearing about the value of education, not because of the importance of learning, the ability to discover new things that will unfold the potential in creation, or even because of the role education can play in shaping us for life in this world. Instead, we see education valued because it can lead to a good job, which, in turn, will provide financial stability and security for our future.

Ambition and security get twisted together when we look to ourselves, to our achievements, to our wealth, or even to our reputation for security and safety. Regardless of what we tell ourselves or others on Sunday, we can tell what we trust to make us secure when our security is threatened. We know where our idols are when they are attacked.

Security and peace are part of the promise of the land, but the land itself cannot ultimately deliver on that promise. The land can give partial peace, partial security, and partial stability. The land is meant to point ahead to Jesus Christ, our true peace, our true refuge, and the solid rock upon which we stand.

Our homes, our jobs, and even our families can only give us partial security in this world. Homes can be lost. Jobs can end. Families can break. None of these things can bear the weight of our need for peace and security. Whenever we try to make them more than they are meant to be, they strain under the weight. Home is never quite what we hoped, so ambition leads us to look for something else. Work becomes toil, so we start daydreaming of a better job. As Jonathan Wilson-Hartgrove puts it, "When we are frustrated by life's difficulties, afraid we're not measuring up, ambition whispers, "Maybe you're not doing what you were made for. Maybe your talent could shine brighter if you were doing something else.""[2]

These attempts at security can be ways of forgetting God. When we believe our stability lies in a good education, a good job, or even a good marriage, we might need God to get us there, but once we have arrived, we no longer need him. We have what we thought would bring us peace, so, as thankful as we are for God getting us there, we believe that we can take it from here. Wilson-Hartgrove again: "Awareness of vainglory's delusion reminds us to ask how much of the stability we invest in — good education, stable jobs, and even our ideal of family — is an attempt to establish security for ourselves apart from dependence on another's grace? If we are to practice true stability, we must find ways to receive it over and again as a gift. Rich or poor, we cannot get away from our fundamental need for a home in the household of God."[3] True stability is found in Jesus Christ. All attempts to find security somewhere else are bound to end in disappointment and breed forgetfulness of the Lord.

Obedience as Avoidance: Ironically, we can be most forgetful of God when we are most vigilant about obeying him. Like Jonah, we can use the command of the Lord to avoid the presence of the Lord.[4] Commitments in the church can pile up and we can convince ourselves that we are alright, even though we have not prayed in weeks. We use 'working for the Lord' as a means of avoiding his presence. On the outside, everything can be clean and in order, but inwardly we continue to run from God.

Just as we cannot avoid sin by running from community into the desert, we also cannot avoid sin simply by following all the external rules. Monks and nuns who have left the world and entered a monastery often find it easy to fall prey to spiritual pride and performance. Where everyone is committed to following God as much as possible, even obedience can become a show or a competition. Herman Bavinck says, "It is precisely the history of asceticism that is best calculated to cure us of the error that sin can be overcome by asceticism. People take their hearts with them when they enter a monastery, and from the heart arise all sorts of sins and iniquities."[5] We cannot outrun our selves and we cannot outrun God.

Obedience to God is good. Faithfulness is good. Service

and activity are good. But even these good things can become twisted into means of keeping God at arm's length. Self-righteousness often masks itself as righteousness. We can try to do all the right things in order to avoid having to slow down and deal with God. Like Israel, we may acknowledge God with our lips, but our hearts are far from him (Isa 29:13; Mt 15:8). Like Jonah, we might be confident that we know exactly what the LORD will say, and want nothing to do with it (Jonah 4:1-3).

Jesus himself warned us that "Not everyone who says to me, 'Lord, Lord,' will enter the kingdom of heaven, but only the one who does the will of my Father who is in heaven. Many will say to me on that day, 'Lord, Lord, did we not prophesy in your name and in your name drive out demons and in your name perform many miracles?' Then I will tell them plainly, 'I never knew you. Away from me, you evildoers!'" (Mt 7:21-23). Those who enter the kingdom will be those who walk according to the will of the Father. However, Jesus names the possibility that people can do all sorts of good in his name, but never know him.

Jesus has a word for us when faith becomes a performance, and when our obedience transforms from service to God to posturing before others:

> Be careful not to practice your righteousness in front of others to be seen by them. If you do, you will have no reward from your Father in heaven.
>
> So when you give to the needy, do not announce it with trumpets, as the hypocrites do in the synagogues and on the streets, to be honored by others. Truly I tell you, they have received their reward in full. But when you give to the needy, do not let your left hand know what your right hand is doing, so that your giving may be in secret. Then your Father, who sees what is done in secret, will reward you.
>
> And when you pray, do not be like the hypocrites, for

they love to pray standing in the synagogues and on the street corners to be seen by others. Truly I tell you, they have received their reward in full. But when you pray, go into your room, close the door and pray to your Father, who is unseen. Then your Father, who sees what is done in secret, will reward you. And when you pray, do not keep on babbling like pagans, for they think they will be heard because of their many words. Do not be like them, for your Father knows what you need before you ask him. (Matt 6:1-8).

We can turn obedience into a spectacle. We can turn our desires from loving and serving God to being seen by our neighbors. We can survive on this strategy of external obedience until suffering opens up a rift in our hearts. Suddenly, all the strategies we have used to keep ourselves going start to sputter. We begin to resonate with Dante, who opens his Divine Comedy with these lines:

> Midway along the journey of our life
> I awoke to find myself in a dark wood,
> For I had wandered off from the straight path.[6]

We may be comfortable in our home, in sending our kids to a good school, and even by being part of a healthy church, but we find ourselves in a dark wood because, for all our running and pushing and doing for God, we are lost. We try to fix our restless wandering by doing more. We commit ourselves to a more rigorous devotional routine. We sign up for another Bible study. We start serving meals to others. All good things — but rearranging the externals does not get to the rootlessness in our hearts.

When Pastor Eugene Peterson entered a season of life he came to call "the Badlands," he awoke to his own forgetfulness of God. "Gradually it dawned on me that the crevasse was not before me but within me. Things were worse than I had supposed; this was requiring more attention than I had planned on."[7]

A crevasse can open between what we say with our lips or do with our hands and what resides in our heart. Service can abound while prayer languishes. All *should* be right, but we sense that nothing is quite right and our restless search starts again. We have entered the land of forgetfulness.

Self-made people: We can forget God even as we post a picture of our coffee and bible (#coffeeandjesus) on Instagram. The contemporary world forces each of us to take part in the individual project of creating our own identities. These self-made identities must be signaled or expressed in order to be real.

Think of how often we feel the need to put a banner on our Facebook profile picture, use a particular hashtag on Twitter, or put a sign on our lawn. If we do not publicly signal our virtue in these ways, we fear that many will believe us uncaring and vicious, regardless of what we do privately. Even as we seek to form our own identities through personal choices, branding, and beliefs, we live in a world where every belief is contested. We may believe wholeheartedly that Jesus rose from the dead, but we know that it is one option among many. That changes how we hold our beliefs. Even the most strident atheist or believer lives with the possibility that he or she could be wrong, however small they believe that possibility may be. As Alan Noble says, "Part of the reason we can hold our beliefs so lightly is that what is truly important to us is not only or primarily our beliefs, but how they affect our identity."[8]

In the context of competing (and even contradictory)

beliefs, faith in Christ can easily be reduced to a lifestyle choice. The cultural water in which we swim can lead us to make even our faith in Christ about *us*. Even if we are certain Christianity is the best life choice, it is still a life choice, an "identity" we choose, a part of our personal brand. Everything in life, including God, becomes part of our project of creating ourselves. Everything orbits around us at the center. Other people become appendices to our story, our brand, our universe. Even God is removed from being the Lord of the universe and relegated to a line on our profile page.

We are continually tempted to live as if *our* story is what really matters, as if we are at the center of the drama, and our actions are what will really last. We need to re-size our vision. As J. Todd Billings says, "We need to realize how little we apprehend, how little we control — how our ambitions are usually out of proportion to our tiny, creaturely lives, and how the everlasting Lord is the only one worthy of our ultimate hopes."[9] We need to respond to the smallness of our lives with humility and love, not by inflating our own importance.

This project of making ourselves leads us to prize a certain kind of authenticity. Being authentic is seen as taking what is inside of us and expressing it in the world. We strive to "be true to ourselves", which is a way of saying that we are seek integrity or congruence between what is in our heart and mind and what we do with our lives and show to the world. There is something right about this — we should live with integrity between belief and action, body and soul. We have already talked about the dangers that come when a gap opens up between our external actions for God and our internal forgetfulness of God.

However, in our modern context, authenticity has lost any reference outside of ourselves. What are we supposed to be authentic *to*? Authenticity is about being true. It is about integrity. Yet, genuine authenticity is about being true to the

Truth, to the God who has made us for himself and made our hearts to rest in him. Authenticity is about having our whole selves working with the grain of God's design and will, instead of having a part of us going one way and a part going another. Having lost a sense of God and of the common good in our society, we now lack the ability to name the truth in light of which we are called to live. We cannot name what an authentic life looks like, so we all define it for ourselves. Authenticity has become being true to how we (individually) experience and feel, not to the way things are or should be.

Authenticity, in today's usage, is not only grounded in experience, but true authenticity *requires* experience. If we have not gone through the struggle ourselves, have not reached the crisis and come out the other side, we don't believe we can claim to have had an authentic existence. No matter how much the church rails against relativism and the "squishy morality" of the world, we can be just as captive to this kind of thinking as anyone else. Consider how we often view those who have grown up in the bosom of the church and never experienced a crisis of doubt or walked away from the church. Many Christians view that faith as less real than those who had to 'claim it for themselves.'

Alan Noble gets it right: "In other words, being raised from childhood into belief in Christ is suspicious, somehow less genuine, and certainly more susceptible to falling away because the alternatives have not been considered. Rather than seeing faithfulness from birth to death as a blessing from God (which is certainly the model of the Old Testament), we harbor doubts about such believers' sincerity."[10]

In college, I spent a summer as a camp counselor at a Christian camp. During staff training, we were all asked to share our testimony. I began to notice something as we made our way around the room. Those who grew up in stable homes, loving Jesus, and faithfully going to church, were embarrassed that they didn't have 'as good a testimony' as others. No one said it directly, but we implicitly knew that 'growing up faithfully in the church' was not good enough. We needed to make sure everyone knew our faith was genuine and not something we inherited from our parents.

There is more than one story of God's faithfulness. God is faithful to save when he calls those living in darkness to cling to Christ in faith and grow into maturity. But God is also faithful to save when he nurtures children in the faith and leads them to cling to Christ and grow into maturity.

Whatever the story, God is the primary actor in the story, not us. In the exodus and in the wilderness, it is clear that God is walking large upon the stage of history. There is no mistaking who the story is about. Exodus is a God story first, then an Israel story. Upon entering the land, Israel is tempted to shift themselves to center stage and give God the bit piece on the side. But life in the land, life in the church, is just as much a God story as life in the wilderness. We have our place, but on the side of the stage, not in the center.

Forgetting each other: In this land of forgetfulness, we not only forget God, but we forget one another. Both love of God and love of neighbor shrivel when love of self reigns supreme. As Todd Billings notes, the sense of control our technology brings often increases our ability to forget others in favor of our own projects and plans. "Our talismans of mastery, such as the smartphone, remind us of our busy schedules. They *don't* remind us of the lonely grandfather sitting at home or the dying member of our congregation who can no longer make it to Sunday services."[11]

When we view everything in light of our own brand and our own story, people who do not serve the story we are making can quickly be forgotten. Cultivating our image often means cutting people out. Climbing to the top often means trampling on the backs of the people who once walked alongside us. People become expendable. Forgetting others may happen in large and cruel ways, but it may also happen in small subtle ways. The phone calls become less frequent. The birthdays are forgotten. What are his kids' names again?

Israel's time in the land of forgetfulness results not only in idolatry, but in injustice. They not only forget God, but begin to use, abuse, and exploit one another. The prophets are a consistent witness to the relationship between the people's neglect of the Lord and their wicked treatment of each other (Mic 2-3). This wickedness could take place while they are doing all the right things in worship (Isa 58).

Just like the Israelites, we select those who fit with our values, our project, and our story, and we ignore the rest. Wilson-Hartgrove gives this practice a name: infidelity. "The great advantage of a Facebook friendship, of course, is that it is so easy. I get to choose who I want to "friend" and whose friendship requests I respond to. We gather around our common interests, share the stuff we want others to know, and log off when we feel like it. In many ways what we have is connection without obligation. But intimacy without commitment is what our society has traditionally called "infidelity.""[12] When we forget God and forget one another, all in the service of ourselves, this is true infidelity.

GRATITUDE: ENJOYING CREATION WITH AN OPEN HAND

How we do not fall prey to the temptation to forgetfulness? What did Israel neglect that moved it down the path to forgetfulness? "When you have eaten and are satisfied, praise the LORD your God for the good land he has given you." (Deut 8:

10). They neglected praise. They did not turn toward God in gratitude.

Living rooted calls for intentional gratitude to God. We need a double movement — we need to turn our eyes from ourselves to creation and behold the beauty and abundance there, enjoying it and rejoicing in it. Then we need to turn toward God in thanksgiving.

It is good to enjoy creation. The beauty of a sunset, the feeling of sand between our toes, and the sound of rain pattering on our roof are all to be enjoyed as gifts from God. Even human achievements can be enjoyed with thanksgiving: the stunning architecture of a gothic cathedral, the power and precision of a dancer, or the wonder of discovery. In fact, it is an act of ingratitude to look out at creation and not be thankful. It is important, though, to pay attention *to whom* we direct our gratitude.

Beauty often breaks through the cracks of our self-protection, pulling back the veil to reveal that we live in a world of wonder, a world that is never completely in our control. This is why even self-avowed atheists can attest to moments of transcendence before the beauty of the cosmos, even if they are not sure what to do with the emotion.

Living rooted involves this double movement, where we enjoy creation as given to us, but also turn around and give thanks to God. We see and enjoy creation as it points to the Creator. We delight in the world, not as an end in itself, but as it leads us to delight in God.

When we enjoy creation without gratitude, we end up putting more pressure on it than it was meant to bear. Everything we put our hope in other than God will ultimately fall short. All these substitutes for God will disappoint us and, in the end, destroy us — or we will destroy them. We cannot expect films, television shows, art, or anything else to fill our souls or keep us rooted. When we do, we set ourselves up for disappointment. James K. A. Smith uses the image of a clenched fist versus an open hand: "It is when I stop over-expecting from creation that it becomes something I can hold with an open hand, lightly but gratefully."[13]

Gratitude enables us to enjoy the world God has given us without clinging too tightly to it. We can relax our grip upon our relationships, our jobs, and our stuff, and give thanks to God. We can loosen our hold on those beautiful moments and places, refusing to squeeze more out of them than we should. We can even hold more lightly our own lives, giving thanks to God for every day, but not holding life with a death grip. Gratitude loosens our grip on the world so that we can properly enjoy it. Gratitude to God gives us peace and serves to draw us away from forgetfulness into faithful remembrance.

Paul speaks of it this way in Philippians 4:

> Rejoice in the Lord always. I will say it again: Rejoice! Let your gentleness be evident to all. The Lord is near. Do not be anxious about anything, but in every situation, by prayer and petition, with thanksgiving, present your requests to God. And the peace of God, which transcends all understanding, will guard your hearts and your minds in Christ Jesus.
>
> Finally, brothers and sisters, whatever is true, whatever is noble, whatever is right, whatever is pure, whatever is lovely, whatever is admirable—if anything is excellent or praiseworthy—think about such things. (Phil 4:4-8)

We are called to rejoice in thanksgiving to God. As a result, we have peace, our anxiety drains away, and we can then consider all the good things of creation. In our daily lives, simple acts like saying grace before meals or observing the sabbath direct our hearts to find rest and peace in God. By remembering God's goodness in the ordinary places of life, our quests for security, the masks of obedience we employ as a way of avoiding God, the myth that we can make ourselves by our choices, and our self-absorption all begin to fade away. When we are rooted in our Creator, we stop expecting creation to do more than it was made to do.

As James K. A. Smith notes, the security of God's love cuts through all our desires to perform. "To aspire to friendship with God, however, is an ambition for something you could never lose. It is to get attention from someone who sees you and knows you and will never stop loving you. In short, it's the opposite of fickle human attention, which is temporal and temperamental. God's attention is not predicated on your performance. You don't have to catch God's notice with your display."[14] When we know our Creator loves us, we can stop the performance and find our rest in him.

For Israel, entering the land comes with its own dangers. Entering the land itself is not enough to inoculate them from the temptation to forget God. Over and over again, they receive the blessings of God and, instead of thanking him, they become proud of their own achievements. This leads to the steady decline of Israel and to their movement into exile.

We, too, face the temptation to forget God. As we seek to be rooted in a mobile world, we can do all the right things, living local and earthy, and yet find ourselves forgetting God. We can forget Him without ever consciously denying him or changing our beliefs. We do this whenever we attempt to shove God to the side and place ourselves or our desires at the center. This forgetfulness can hide in the quest for security and safety, can show up in a zeal for obedience, or can even become part of our brand, a lifestyle choice that enhances "the story of me."

The antidote to forgetfulness is gratitude. When we stop and intentionally take time to thank God for the good gifts of creation, we will hold this world more lightly and hold on to God more tightly. This enables us to enjoy the land God has given us and the place where he has put us, without expecting it to do more than it was made to do.

UPROOTED

They shall be like a tree planted by water,
Sending out its roots by the stream.
It shall not fear when heat comes,
And its leaves shall stay green;
In the year of drought it is not anxious,
And it does not cease to bear fruit
Jeremiah 17:8 NRSV

5

GO FROM YOUR COUNTRY

OUR LANDLESS FATHERS AND MOTHERS

Late capitalism is the age in which everyone has a computer in their pocket and a gaping hole where a father should be.
- James K. A. Smith

Abram lives an exodus-shaped life, from beginning to end.
- Alastair Roberts & Andrew Wilson

As I lowered the hood of the grill, I noticed Aaron walking down the street. Probably sixteen years old, he often walked back and forth down my street in the late afternoon. He usually stopped by to talk when I was grilling. I could hear his headphones as he walked over. We talked about music for a while, then the discussion turned to school. I asked about his plans after graduation.

"I don't know. I just want to live restless, you know?"

"I'm not sure I do. Could you tell me what you mean?"

"I just don't want to be stuck where I am. Tied down. I feel restless, like I need to go and be somewhere else. Somewhere not here. I just want to live restless."

He wanted to "live restless." It was more than wanting to

move out of the house or make his own decisions. These are typical feelings of teenagers approaching adulthood. He wanted to communicate more. He *was* restless. I could see it in his body language. But he wanted to *live* restless. I felt exhausted for him already.

Our culture lives with a deep restlessness, a deep rootlessness that stretches back to our exile from Eden. Our mobile culture invites us to be constantly on the move, to let our restless anxiety fuel creativity and productivity. However, more and more of us live on the edge of burnout or something worse. Most of us cannot go back to a simpler life, nor would we always want to. Yet, we must find a different pathway through the complex, restless world in which we live.

God's people know what it means to be rootless in the world. God promised land, but he also repeatedly called his people out of their lands to follow him. Held by God's promises, his people could live as sojourners without living restless.

To see this, we will need to spend time in the story of Abraham and his children, because there are similarities between the vulnerable rootlessness in our society and the experience of the patriarchs. God calls his people to leave behind everything they have known. As God's people on foreign soil, they live with vulnerability and contention everywhere they go. However, Augustine echoes the biblical story when he says: "Nevertheless, to praise you is the desire of man, a little piece of your creation. You stir man to take pleasure in praising you, because you have made us for yourself, and our heart is restless until it rests in you."[1]

UPROOTED BY GOD'S CALL

Sometimes God uproots us before he plants us.

God promises Abram land and offspring. He tells him to

look out across Canaan and behold the land that he will give his descendants. He tells them that they will be rooted in the land and that they will have a place to learn how to love God and love their neighbor. They will have the blessing of being in God's country. But first, Abram must get up and go.

Before Israel can be planted in Canaan, Abram must be uprooted from his homeland. Abram's father, Terah, had three sons: Abram, Nahor, and Haran. After Abram and Nahor both got married (and after Haran died), the whole family packed up and moved from Ur of the Chaldeans. Ur was one of the great cities of that day. Sitting at the mouth of the Euphrates river, this coastal city was powerful. It was a center of trade and culture. The family traveled hundreds of miles up the Euphrates river to the region that would be called Haran (possibly named after Terah's dead son, Haran). In modern geography, Terah, Abram, and their families left southern Iraq and traveled all the way up into Turkey.

Haran may have been a better place for the family to live than Ur. It may have made sense as a place to settle. Yet we have no indication that the family was following God's call by moving to Haran. They were heading the right direction (toward the land of Canaan), but they were probably doing it for their own reasons.

Abram's next move is different, though. God tells Abram, "Go from your country, your people, and your father's household to the land I will show you" (Gen 12:1). The LORD calls Abram to make a complete break from his past and his identity.

Some of us know what it feels like to leave our home country for a new one. Some of us have paid the cost of following Jesus when it cuts us off from our family. The call God issues to Abram is hard. Leaving the land of his birth will be painful. It may even feel a little like a betrayal. In our highly mobile society, we often don't have the same ties to the land that our ancestors once did. However, we can imagine a bit of what Abram is called to give up — his country, his people, his father's household. These relationships define who he is. Even as an adult, he is always "Terah's boy." But God says, "Go from your country, your people, and your father's household to the land I will show you."

Furthermore, God does not even tell Abram where he is sending him. Abram is called to make a complete break with his past without knowing anything about the future. He must trust the God who called him. This is not immigration from the old country to the land of opportunity, but a blind trust in where God will lead him.

Hearing the call of God, Abram goes. "And Abram went as the LORD had told him" (Gen 12:4). There is no indication that Abram takes time to think about God's command or even to discuss it with Sarai, his wife. God speaks and Abram follows. He takes everything — family, livestock, possessions, people. From what we know of the local geography, this is a four-hundred-mile journey.

Abram enters Canaan from the north and travels straight to Shechem, the heart of the land. There, God reveals to him this is the land God will give him. This will be his inheritance and the beachhead of God's work of redeeming the world. Yet, the land is already occupied. There are already people there. In fact, Shechem is one of the centers of worship for the Canaanite religion. There are people there and they are already worshipping *their* gods. Nonetheless, God promises to give this land to Abram's descendants. So, in the center of the land, most likely in full view of the Canaanite shrine, Abram builds an altar to the LORD.

Abram then moves south to Bethel and again builds an altar to the LORD, near another center of Canaanite religion. It is only after Abram enters the land God will give him, and only when he is in that land, that Abram builds these altars to the LORD.

Abram's movement through the land is as much about spiritual geography as it is about physical geography. Building an altar is both an act of worship and a proclamation that this land belongs to God. Abram is praising God and reclaiming the land for the LORD. Just as Noah built an altar after the flood, proclaiming God's rule over the earth, Abram's altars are like raising a flag over the land of Canaan. Wherever God has given Abram land, Abram claims it for the LORD. As John Calvin says, Abram "endeavoured, as much as lay in him, to dedicate to God, every part of the land to which he had access, and perfumed it with the odor of his faith.[2]" Abram does not claim the land through force or conquest, but through worship. He lifts high the name of the LORD where the world is watching.

SOJOURNING PEOPLE: VULNERABILITY

Yet, as soon as Abram builds these altars and claims that this land belongs to the LORD, he is forced to leave Canaan. By Genesis 12:10, the land of promise has become a land of emptiness. This place of blessing is in the midst of a famine. This must be a difficult early test for Abram. God has promised him a good land, but it clearly isn't good now. Instead of immediate prosperity, God's promises are followed by hardship.

Abram then goes down to Egypt to live because Egypt depends less on rainfall and more on irrigation, and is, therefore, less susceptible to famine. The word used for 'live' means 'to live as a stranger.' Abram is not moving to Egypt or taking up permanent residence there. Instead, he is a stranger, an alien, a sojourner.

However, in Egypt, Abram and Sarai are vulnerable. They

are wealthy and powerful enough to be known by Pharaoh, but their status is unsure. As foreigners, they have little to no rights. They cannot call for justice in the same way as the native Egyptians and can thus be easily exploited. (The same was true much later, as Paul appealed to his own Roman citizenship on multiple occasions. Roman citizens also had rights that foreigners did not have).

Abram fears that their status as outsiders will lead them to be exploited, so he concocts a plan: Sarai will claim to be his sister. In that time period, a suitor approached the brother (or father) of a woman he wished to marry. If Abram is seen as Sarai's husband, he is an obstacle to be removed to get Sarai. If he is her brother, though, he is someone who must be appeased in order to get Sarai's hand. Abram's plan raises all sorts of interesting questions, which we will not address here. However, the fact that Abram and Sarai need to devise a plan at all, even something as risky as this, suggests just how vulnerable they are.

Everything happens almost exactly as Abram has predicted. Sarai's beauty becomes public knowledge and she gains Pharaoh's attention. As a man who takes whatever he wants, Pharaoh takes Sarai into his palace. Abram is treated well, gaining much livestock and many servants, so much that he leaves Egypt richer than when he arrived. But Sarai is taken by Pharaoh, who, we learn later, intends to take her as his wife.

Surprisingly, Abram does nothing. We are not told why. He may be selfish, he may be indifferent, or he may desperately want to rescue her, but feel powerless to do so. For whatever reason, Abram does nothing.

Yet, God is not idle. "But the LORD inflicted serious diseases on Pharaoh and his household because of Abram's wife, Sarai" (Gen 12:17). God sends plagues upon Pharaoh and his family in the form of disease, perhaps in part to prevent Pharaoh from consummating his marriage to Sarai.

God brings his judgment on Pharaoh and rescues Sarai. The diseases are so severe that Pharaoh does everything in his power to get Abram and Sarai to leave the country. "Then he gave orders about Abram to his men and they sent him on his way, with his wife and everything he had" (Gen 12:20).

Abram and Sarai are sojourners. They are aliens in the land of Canaan and in the land of Egypt. "They are the people of sojourn. Sojourner is a technical world usually described as "resident alien." It means to be in a place, perhaps for an extended time, to live there and take some roots, but always to be an outsider, never belonging, always without rights, title, or voice in decisions that matter."[3] Their life and existence are vulnerable because they live *in* a place, but do not *belong* there.

This vulnerability is a consistent pattern for Abraham (previously Abram) and his descendants. Twice Abraham attempts to pass off Sarah (previously Sarai) as his sister instead of his wife and both times it almost leads to disaster. Once Isaac did the same with Rebekah. Every time, it is not the people's cleverness, but the Lord's hand, that protected those in peril.

Yet, they are vulnerable in the land. Abraham is called out of the land again and again, spending as much time outside the land as within it. Twice he rescues his nephew Lot, who lives outside the land. Even when Sarah dies, because they have no plot of land where they can bury her, Abraham must negotiate to purchase the burial plot at Mamre. Everywhere he goes, Abraham is vulnerable. His life always seems to hang in the balance, but remains held firmly by the LORD.

SOJOURNING PEOPLE: CONFLICT

Sometimes God uproots us before he plants us. Consider Abraham's son, Isaac, who struggles for years in Gerar — outside the promised land. Like his father before him (and his son after him), Isaac is forced to leave because of famine. Like his father before him, Isaac experiences a form of exile. The land will not support him and he is thrust out into the world of the nations.

As Isaac leaves the land and travels to Gerar, the LORD appears to him and tells him not to go down to Egypt. Earlier, Abraham went there during a famine, and later the family of Jacob will also go there, but God does not want Isaac in Egypt. Perhaps Egypt will be too much of a temptation for Isaac; perhaps Gerar is enough of a challenge for him. Maybe the LORD has plans for Isaac in Gerar — to bear witness to the LORD before the Philistines. Regardless, God tells Isaac to stay in Gerar. God promises to be with Isaac, to bless and multiply him there.

As Pharaoh once sought Sarai, Abimelech (the king of Gerar) now seeks Isaac's wife, Rebekah. As Abram did with Sarai, Isaac passes Rebekah off as his sister, and she is threatened, just as Sarai was. Yet, by God's grace, Rebekah is protected. Abimelech warns the whole nation to touch neither Rebekah nor Isaac.

After this initial challenge, Isaac experiences blessing in Gerar. He plants and reaps a hundredfold. He grows rich through God's blessing. Unfortunately, this sparks jealousy. The Philistines stop up the wells that Abraham dug, destroying Abraham's legacy and preventing the land from being fruitful for Isaac. Eventually, even King Abimelech drives Isaac away when Isaac becomes too powerful.

Isaac then leaves the city and settles in the valley below. He begins to re-dig the wells the Philistines had filled. After this, he digs three more wells, which he names Esek, Sitnah, and Rehoboth. By digging these wells, Isaac is opening up the land to be fruitful. The wells have been plugged, preventing the animals and crops from getting the water and irrigation they need. Now, Isaac opens the wells again so the blessings of water flow. He pours out blessing and restores the name of his father, Abraham, by digging his father's wells again. He does not work to make his own name great, but to elevate the name of his father. He does not hoard God's blessings, but pours out blessing in a land not his own — Gerar. Even when the people quarrel with him, Isaac keeps on digging. He does not let their opposition keep him from being a blessing.

Isaac goes to Gerar, where he faces threats against his wife, Rebekah, as well as false accusations, and much envy. He is eventually driven out and the Philistines quarrel with him over his family's wells. He faces challenges and opposition at nearly every turn, yet God blesses him. He pours out that blessing from God by digging wells so that the land will prosper. God promised Abraham that he and his children would be blessed and would be a blessing to the nations. We begin to see the realization of that promise through the life of Isaac.

Yet, Isaac remains a sojourner. God blesses and protects him in that place, but Isaac does not truly belong. He faces contention, jealousy, and challenges on every side. Though he does nothing wrong, he is forced out of the city. Though the wells belonged to his father, Isaac is forced over and over again to move on and to dig again. "To an observer, the sojourner-pilgrim is just there, coping and surviving. Perhaps only the insider can know that he is not just "being there," but is on his way toward a promise."[4]

At the heart of the sojourning life, there is a kind of root-lessness. God's people will have the land, they will receive the promise, but they do not *belong* to the land. They always remain outsiders and vulnerable. Abraham's descendants receive the promise, but still live as sojourners. Their relationship with the inhabitants of the land is frequently strained and always tenuous.

They live in Canaan, but are not to become one with the land's inhabitants. Abraham looks for a wife for Isaac, not among the inhabitants of the land, but from his own family back in Haran. Isaac's son, Esau, marries two Canaanite women, who make life bitter for Isaac and Rebekah (Gen 26:35). Jacob is sent to Haran as well to find a wife from Rebekah's family (27:41ff.).

Later, the inhabitants of the land propose a merger between the people of Jacob and the inhabitants of Shechem. Dinah, Jacob's daughter, has been raped and her brothers use the marriage proposal as a means of revenge. They ask the men of the town to be circumcised, like true sons of Abraham. While the men are recovering, the brothers slaughter the whole town. When Jacob hears what his sons have done, he does not immediately voice concern for his daughter, Dinah, but for how this action will put the entire family in a vulnerable place. "Then Jacob said to Simeon and Levi, "You have brought trouble on me by making me odious to the inhabitants of the land, the Canaanites and the Perizzites; my numbers are few, and if they gather themselves against me and attack me, I shall be destroyed, both I and my household"" (34:30). The family is vulnerable and Jacob's sons have put them all in danger.

Jacob himself spends decades outside of the land. He tarries in Laban's house until he is trapped. His labor is exploited for years and his wages change repeatedly. Through it all, though, God continues to bless Jacob, even as Laban cheats him. After returning from Laban's house, Jacob has a fearful confrontation with Esau that ends in reconciliation. Yet, Jacob does not follow Esau back to his home. Instead, he settles instead in Sukkoth, east of the Jordan, outside of the land.

Jacob's favored son, Joseph, also lives as a sojourner. Sold into slavery, Joseph lives as a foreigner in Egypt, where he is a vulnerable slave, falsely accused and thrown into prison. Even when he is elevated, Joseph has a precarious relationship with Pharaoh. Sometimes God uproots us before he plants us.

Central to the book of Genesis and the life of the patriarchs is the promise of the land. However, the patriarchs spend very little time in the land they are promised. The land cannot support them, they are hated by its inhabitants, or they are tempted to assimilate to the ways of the people of the land. They are constantly on the move. "The land is referred to as the "land of sojourning," the place where they are but do not belong and do not have rootage."[5] They live in Haran, Canaan, Gerar, and Egypt — and places in between. In every place, they are vulnerable, their status and relationship to the broader culture and powers unsure. They consistently run the risk of being exploited and of enduring injustice.

Yet, these are the people called by God. God calls Abram to leave his land of origin, to leave the place he is from and enter into rootlessness. As much as we may rightly lament living rootless, the people of God know this as both a sorrow and as a calling from God. "Instead of hallowing the land of origin, God was continually calling his people out of lands, dragging them across the desert like a nomadic dreamer, to inherit his territorial estate. Yet not even this land was God's ultimate dwelling place."[6] God takes Abraham (and his descendants) out of the land in order to bring them home to himself. But first, they must spend some time as sojourners.

ABRAHAMIC ROOTLESSNESS

Christians know the fragility and vulnerability of rootlessness all too well. Leaving everything behind to follow God's call is not unique to Abram. Christians have crossed oceans, left family, left jobs, and entered the vulnerable life of sojourners to go where God leads them. Christians have left safety, security, and comfort behind for unknown lands, unknown futures, and unknown tasks because God called them. Like Abram before us, we have heard the voice of God calling us to get up and go, to leave behind even what is most precious to us, and to go where God will show us. At times, our faith feels like stepping out over a chasm, trusting God will place our feet on solid ground.

This experience of God's call continues in the life of the church. The desert fathers and mothers leave cities to go into the wilderness. The North African Augustine lives in Rome and Milan. The Frenchman Calvin lives and serves in Geneva. The saints often live as foreigners in a strange land. *Sometimes God uproots us before he plants us.*

Yet, this Abrahamic rootlessness differs significantly from the rootlessness so prevalent in our culture. Abram steps out in faith, trusting in the promise of God. He and his descendants live without the security of stable homes, citizenship, or worldly belongings because they belong to God and have their eyes on his promise. They are people on a pilgrimage, walking toward a country they cannot see.

Our culture is committed to wandering, not pilgrimage. We have no destination in sight. The rootlessness we feel in the West is not driven by the longing for the promised land. Our culture does not ache because we anticipate the coming kingdom. We ache because we are not at home and have no idea where to go.

As James K. A. Smith describes it, "ours is a pilgrimage without a destination — which is to say, it's not a pilgrimage at all but rather a pilgrimage deferred, not because we stay home but because we revel in the roaming, or at least try to talk ourselves into that."[7] This land is not our home, but we fear that we might not have a home where we can go.

When I lived in Iowa, there was a local cultural practice, known as 'cruising.' Young people would gather on a Saturday night to drive up and down the city's main streets. They had no destination. In fact, a destination would have ruined the experience. Instead, they got together in their cars, rolled down the windows, turned up the music, and just started driving. The journey — the drive — was the point.

Whatever we think about driving aimlessly on a Saturday night, this picture captures more than the habits of Iowa teenagers. This is symbolic of life in the contemporary West. Not just with our cars, but with our lives, we drive with no destination. We live without an end or goal in sight. Without a destination, there is only the journey.

For many of us, the journey becomes the point. As Smith says, "We're always on the move, restless, vaguely chasing something rather than oriented to a destination."[8] It does not matter where we are going — all that matters is who is going with us — or so we tell ourselves. It is not the destination that matters, but the journey we take to get there. We put these slogans on our motivation posters, hoping the words will quiet the unrest in our hearts. However, *where* we are going matters as much as *how* we get there. Our life has a destination. Even if we claim just to be 'enjoying the journey,' we are aiming our life in a particular direction. Claiming our life has no destination does not make it true. It simply means we are not paying attention to where we are going. In the words of James K. A. Smith, "Disordered love is like falling in love with the boat rather than the destination."[9]

For others, "no destination" means making our own goals, determining our own destination. We can be in control and put the right coordinates into the GPS of our life to get where we want to go. We can all make of our lives whatever we choose. This is ultimate freedom, right?

Conversely, instead of freedom and peace, we find that this lack of destination leads to crippling anxiety. How can we know we have made the right choice? What if we make a mistake and end up at the wrong destination? What if we get to the end of our lives and realize that we should have been going somewhere else all along? The virtually endless choices paralyze many of us or prevent us from committing fully to a single path or a specific person, just in case we have to (or want to) make a shift later in life. External factors, such as economic and political uncertainty, significant debt, or past trauma can make the weight of these choices even heavier.

In some ways, our current cultural challenges can be compared with those of Abraham and his descendants. Our culture's rootlessness shares a sense of vulnerability with Abrahamic rootlessness. One brick crumbles and it feels like our whole lives are falling down. Our culture also shares a general feeling with Abraham and his descendants of not being at home in the world. We can be in a place for years and never quite feel like we fit in, like we never quite belong. However, our culture's solutions only delay or deny the problem. We either pretend that rootlessness is normal and good or we try to make something of ourselves *by ourselves*. Either way, we are left on our own to make meaning out of a meaningless world.

However much it may look superficially similar to our cultural challenges, though, Abraham's rootlessness is completely different in character. It is the rootlessness in the world that comes from finding our firm foundation in God. It is the ability to walk unencumbered in this world because our vision is captured by the promise of dwelling with God. Abram leaves everything and walks as a sojourner for all his days, not because there is no destination and he might as well make the best of the journey, but because he has heard the voice of the Lord. Abraham can keep moving and never set down roots in this life because his roots are in the kingdom of God.

The solution, then, to the rootlessness we experience in our world is to find our home — our roots — in God. "Imagine a refugee spirituality, an understanding of human longing and estrangement that not only honors those experiences of not-at-home-ness but also affirms the hope of finding a home, finding oneself...the goal isn't returning home but being welcomed home in a place you weren't born, arriving in a strange land and being told, "You belong here.""[10]

God called Abram and still calls us today to leave everything and follow him. "As Jesus was walking beside the Sea of Galilee, he saw two brothers, Simon called Peter and his brother Andrew. They were casting a net into the lake, for they were fishermen. "Come, follow me," Jesus said, "and I will send you out to fish for people." At once they left their nets and followed him." (Mt 4:18-20).

All we have talked about in the first section of this book on being rooted still holds true. Being rooted in place is important and many of us will find our rootedness in Christ by remaining right where we are. We will cultivate peace in Jesus by rejecting our culture's narrative of restless wandering as the only way of life. However, if we neglect the calling of God to leave, we will miss half the story.

Abram and his descendants are called to leave, to forgo all the comforts of being rooted in the land, and to embark on a life of vulnerability and conflict. Abram and Sarai, Isaac and Rebekah, Jacob and his family all live much of their lives outside the land of promise. They are exploited, pushed around, and consistently in danger. They are sojourners navigating a world with powerful people seeking to exploit them or push them aside. God blesses, protects, and provides for them along the way, but hardship remains. Even when, like Isaac, they respond by patiently blessing the people around them, they remain vulnerable.

However, their vulnerability, their rootlessness, is not the same as the aimless wandering praised in our society. We often cling to comfort and security as we prize the journey without considering the destination. Yet, our fathers and mothers in the faith lived without the comforts and securities of this life precisely because they found their comfort and security in God. They could leave everything and go where God told them because they trusted God's promise of a home in him.

We can only navigate rootlessness in this world by having our roots in God. "Living restless" has only led us to anxiety, exhaustion, and burnout. Augustine understood this: "Nevertheless, to praise you is the desire of man, a little piece of your creation. You stir man to take pleasure in praising you, because you have made us for yourself, and our heart is restless until it rests in you."[11] We will be restless until we rest in God. Only souls that have found rest in God can be free to leave everything behind, free to go where the destination is unknown or uncertain, free to follow where the Lord leads.

When we follow God's call out of the land and into the life of a sojourner, we experience unexpected intimacy with God in the wilderness.

6

WANDERING BUT NOT LOST

EGYPT, EXODUS, AND WILDERNESS

Wilderness, precarious as it is, is where Yahweh is present.
- Walter Brueggemann

[T]he point of the exodus is not just for Israel to find deliverance from serving the old master. It is for them to find delight in serving the new one.
- Alastair Roberts & Andrew Wilson

Where do we meet with God? When, after generations, God's people look back on the times of greatest closeness to God, what comes to mind? In the Bible, God's people remembered not their time in the land, but their time in the wilderness. Even after entering the land, it was the wilderness that spoke of their deepest time of intimacy.

While we meet with God in the ordinary places of life, we often experience closeness to God in the wilderness places of life. When we are removed from our ordinary and (relatively) comfortable life, God meets with us and draws us near. However, so much of life is structured to convince us that we are secure in ourselves. Even the good places God has given us can become lands of forgetfulness. In these times, God often breaks the false security of our lives in order to call us out of our familiar slaveries into the wilderness of life with him.

Being rooted in the land is a gift, but so is being brought into the wilderness. If we are rooted in the wrong place, it can lead to death. Israel was rooted in Egypt for generations, but this led to slavery and oppression. Like Israel, we live in our own Egypts, places that promise security and safety, but lead to slavery. God brought Israel out of bondage in Egypt and does the same for us when we get caught in our personal Egypts. God's work of uprooting us is the gift of true freedom. For Israel, they knew this through the experience of the Exodus. We experience this as salvation and freedom in Christ. For Israel and for us, the wilderness is where God meets with us and leads us into freedom in his presence. But first he must get us out of Egypt.

EGYPTIAN BONDAGE

Israel's first experience as people rooted and settled in a land is not in Canaan, but in Egypt. "Thus Israel settled in the land of Egypt, in the region of Goshen; and they gained possessions in it, and were fruitful and multiplied exceedingly. " (Gen 47:27). Famine brings the sons of Jacob face-to-face with the brother they sold, Joseph, who is now second-in-command of all Egypt. While God's people had *sojourned* in the promised land, they now *settle* in Egypt. They clung to the promise of God as they lived in the land of Canaan, but they never truly belonged. Now, they put down roots in Egypt. As Walter Brueggemann notes, "In that land [Egypt] Israel did not sojourn; it *dwelt* there, securely settled in."[1]

Egypt turns out to be a land of both prosperity and death. In the days of Joseph, Pharaoh and Egypt were pleasantly disposed toward the people of God. When five of Joseph's brothers were brought before Pharaoh and asked permission to live in the land as aliens, Pharaoh welcomed them, allowing them to settle in the land of Egypt with their entire families (wives, children, grandchildren). He also invited them to take the best and richest part of Egypt: Goshen. They were welcomed with open arms. Pharaoh told Joseph to identify the most capable shepherds among the people of Israel and to appoint them to oversee Pharaoh's own flocks. This made them officers of the crown, with privileges and protections not normally given to foreigners. They were given land and work. Joseph provided them with all they needed to eat, while the rest of the country had to pay for its own food. The people of God were blessed above and beyond the average person upon entering Egypt because of their association with Joseph.

Unfortunately, that blessing does not last. The tides turn between the end of Genesis and the beginning of Exodus. When we open the book of Exodus, we find a ruler in Egypt who does not know Joseph. The privileged position of God's people has been lost and they are now viewed as a threat. Pharaoh's policy has changed, ""Come, let us deal shrewdly with them, or they will increase and, in the event of war, join our enemies and fight against us and escape from the land." Therefore they set taskmasters over them to oppress them with forced labor. They built supply cities, Pithom and Rameses, for Pharaoh" (Ex 1:10-11). The oppression grows worse and worse until Pharaoh orders all newborn boys killed and thrown into the Nile. Egypt, which began as a place of blessing, has turned into a land of slavery and death.

While God's great act of salvation ends with God's people rooted in the land of promise, it begins with God uprooting them from the land of slavery and death. They do not start wandering and lost, but firmly rooted in a land that crushes and oppresses. Their problem is not that they are rootless, but that they are stuck in a land that kills. They are rooted in a land of death.

Yet, as miserable as Egypt is, it provides security and it promises stability. The people of God know where they stand and how things work. They live a land where Pharaoh orders children thrown into the Nile, and where the people are beaten, whipped, and oppressed. Yet, Egypt is also familiar to them.

Psychologist and theologian Chuck DeGroat describes how, over the centuries, Israel became accustomed to the pain of Egypt. "They'd built houses and become accustomed to the highways and back roads of Egypt. Egypt had become home."[2] In the wilderness, the people looked back fondly on Egypt. They longed for those days, quickly forgetting what they were like. "If only we had died by the hand of the LORD in the land of Egypt, when we sat by the fleshpots and ate our fill of bread" (Ex 16:3). How can this be their memory of Egypt, this land where the whips are on their backs and their children are killed?

Egypt is miserable, but it is comfortable. It is not comfortable in the sense that the people lounge around eating meat all day (whatever they think they remember) — it is comfortable because they know how the system works. All the advantages of rootedness are there in Egypt. Because it is irrigated land, not dependent upon rainfall, the food supply is stable. Though the work was miserable, it is steady. Everyone has a job, a home, stability, and security. Yet, it is also slavery.

OUR PERSONAL EGYPTS

Like the Israelites, in our longing for security, we can enter into slavery. This is not unique to ancient Israel. As DeGroat says, "We're all ensnared by the Egypts in our lives and the pharaohs that demand our allegiance."[3] We are made to be rooted, but we can be rooted in things that will harm and destroy us. Money, power, and status can each lead to their own kind of slavery, as we can never have quite enough of them. Even good things — family, work, or freedom — can lead us into slavery when we look to them for security.

DeGroat compares our personal Egypts to addiction. "Follow the trajectory of these simple daily attachments and you'll find a need for security, for safety, for intimacy, for connection, for regularity, for productivity. Go a bit deeper and you'll find that each of these things can even replace God, providing for my deep and desperate neediness without consideration of my deep and desperate neediness as a human being."[4]

These Egypts can be seductive because, in the short term, they seem to deliver on their promises. It feels good, it feels fulfilling, until it doesn't. Then we simply need more. Like an addict, we need more and more until our addiction consumes us. The promotion and increase in income provide increased security and stability for a while, but if we can have just a little bit more, then we will really be secure. If we have a few more followers, one more drink, a little more attention, then it will be enough. Tragically, it never is. Like Israel in Egypt, we experience these things as good at the beginning, but quickly come to be enslaved as we put more and more of our trust in them. These Egypts seem to give life and security and stability, but they ultimately bring only disappointment, destruction, and death.

When we root our lives in the wrong places, we find not freedom, but slavery. When we place our trust in created things instead of the Creator, we find only death. When we look for freedom in the wrong places, we end up trapped in Egypt. James K. A. Smith notes how the ancient wisdom of Augustine speaks to this very contemporary experience:

To read Augustine in the twenty-first century is to gain a vantage point that makes all of our freedom look like addiction. When we imagine freedom only as negative freedom — freedom *from* constraint, hands-off liberty to choose what I want — then our so-called freedom is actually inclined to captivity. When freedom is mere voluntariness, without further orientation or goals, then my choice is just another means by which I'm trying to look for satisfaction. Insofar as I keep choosing to try to find that satisfaction in finite, created things — whether it's sex or adoration or beauty or power — I'm going to be caught in a cycle where I'm more and more disappointed in those things *and* more and more dependent on those things.[5]

Welcome to Egypt — only this is an Egypt of our own making.

EXODUS FREEDOM

From the pit of Egypt, God rescues his people. He ultimately leads them into the promised land and roots them in the place he has set for them, a land of life not death. But first, God leads them out of Egypt. In order to lead them into the promised land, he must first lead them out of where they are. They must first be uprooted so that they can be planted in the soil God has prepared.

However, it will not be easy. Pharaoh (and the pharaohs of today who demand our allegiances) does not let go easily. Moses' appearance before Pharaoh signals that battle has commenced. Pharaoh claims ownership of and power over the people of Israel, but the LORD does not let any other claimants have his people.

As Alastair Roberts and Andrew Wilson point out, behind the physical struggle is a spiritual one. "The exodus is a battle of the gods, in which only one can emerge from the ring victorious."[6] The first encounter signifies the coming battle. Moses' staff is cast down and turns into a snake. Wanting to show their strength and power, the servants of Pharaoh cast down their staves, which turn into snakes as well. Yet Moses' staff swallows up the staves of the Egyptian magicians — an ominous beginning for Pharaoh's battle with the living God.

Ten plagues follow. Through the first few plagues, there is no distinction between the people of God and Egypt. All suffer under the same plague. Additionally, the first few plagues are easily reproduced by the Egyptian magicians, such that they claim that they can match the power of the LORD.

Yet as the plagues progress, the LORD makes a larger and larger distinction between his chosen people and the nation of Egypt. The Israelite's livestock and children are protected. Goshen (where the Israelites live) still sees the sun, while Egypt remains in darkness. Pharaoh's magicians are swiftly overwhelmed. "But when the magicians tried to produce gnats by their secret arts, they could not. Since the gnats were on the people and animals everywhere, the magicians said to Pharaoh, "This is the finger of God." But Pharaoh's heart was hard and he would not listen, just as the LORD had said." (Ex 8:18-19). More than once, Pharaoh claims repentance and promises the people can go, but he always goes back on his word.

In the tenth and final plague, God breaks the power of Pharaoh by killing all the firstborn of Egypt — people and animals — while sparing the Israelites. That night has been commemorated throughout the history of the people of God in the celebration of the Passover. As DeGroat says, this Passover is the path into freedom. "Nothing less than a Passover moment is needed for us to cross into freedom, the honest and vulnerable confession that we cannot overcome our darkest moments without our redeeming, liberating

God."[7] Finally, the people of Israel walk out of Egypt, laden with the spoils of the land.

Even after the people leave, though, Pharaoh pursues them. Yet, God continues to deliver his people. The Israelites cross the Red Sea on dry land, while the chariots and armies of Pharaoh are drowned. From there, God brings his people to Mount Sinai. On that mountain, God gives them true freedom. He frees them not only from Pharaoh and his oppression, but also sets them free to serve God. "The two halves of the exodus — freedom from serving Pharaoh and freedom to serve God — are summarized brilliantly at the start of the first commandment: "I am the LORD your God, who brought you out of the land of Egypt, out of the house of slavery. You shall have no other gods before me.""[8] They are now free *from* Pharaoh and free *for* God.

This is the freedom God gives us in Jesus Christ when he calls us out of our Egypts — freedom *from* sin and death and freedom *for* life in fellowship with God. We were rooted in the land of sin and death, stuck in a bondage we could not escape. Yet the LORD broke the power of sin, death, and the devil, leading his people out of slavery into freedom. "In a sense, the exile from Eden is like Israel's journey *into* Egypt, preparing us for the liberation of God's people, and ultimately his world, from oppression and frustration, which will ultimately be accomplished in Jesus."[9] Like Israel, we must be uprooted before we can be transplanted into the garden of God.

Like the freedom given to Israel at Mount Sinai, the freedom Christ gives us includes constraints. It is both freedom *from* the bondage of sin, but also freedom *for* service to God. As James K. A. Smith notes, freedom and boundaries go together. "We might be surprised by how many people are hoping someone will give them boundaries, the gift of restraint, channeling their desires and thereby shoring up a sense of self."[10] God leads his people out of Egypt to the foot of Mount Sinai. For the fullness of freedom, they need the Red Sea crossing and Mount Sinai. We need to be brought out of bondage (Red Sea), but also directed toward the good of life with God (Mount Sinai). On Mount Sinai, Israel was rooted in their relationship with God. God did not free Israel in order for them to wander, but so they could walk with God.

> Then Moses went up to God, and the LORD called to him from the mountain and said, "This is what you are to say to the descendants of Jacob and what you are to tell the people of Israel: 'You yourselves have seen what I did to Egypt, and how I carried you on eagles' wings and brought you to myself. Now if you obey me fully and keep my covenant, then out of all nations you will be my treasured possession. Although the whole earth is mine, you will be for me a kingdom of priests and a holy nation.' These are the words you are to speak to the Israelites." (Ex 19:3-6).

God brings his people out of Egypt and brings them to himself. They are treasured and cherished, but also called. Not long after these words, God gives his people the Ten Commandments. These commandments are to guide the people in living free with God. The grace of the exodus has set them secure in God. As Smith again notes, this grace is freedom: "it's an invitation to a life that is secure enough to risk, centered enough to be courageous, like the rails of a roller coaster that let you do loop after loop. It's the grace that guards your being, the gift that gives you your self again."[11] The law is not another oppressive yoke, similar to what they had experienced in Egypt, but the way into the freedom of life with God.

WILDERNESS INTIMACY

After being uprooted from Egypt, we are led into the wilderness. Far from being a place of rootlessness, the wilderness is a place of intimacy with God. Having been set free from bondage in Egypt and given the Law to guide their life together, Israel truly needed a period of intimacy with God. It is what our hearts need as well.

However, this is not how most of us remember Israel's time in the wilderness. We remember them grumbling and whining. We remember the golden calf, where they turned away from God. We remember them complaining about manna, complaining about not enough variety of food, complaining about water, and pining to be back in Egypt. Israel remembered this too:

> Today, if only you would hear his voice,
> "Do not harden your hearts as you did at Meribah,
>   as you did that day at Massah in the wilderness,
> where your ancestors tested me;
>   they tried me, though they had seen what I did.
> For forty years I was angry with that generation;
>   I said, 'They are a people whose hearts go astray,
>   and they have not known my ways.'
> So I declared on oath in my anger,
>   'They shall never enter my rest.' (Ps 95:7b-11).

The wilderness is a time of grumbling and complaining, a period of dryness and frustration. However, this is not all that it is. It is also Israel's honeymoon with God. Mount Sinai is like a wedding ceremony where God takes Israel as his bride and the forty years in the wilderness are the honeymoon. Yes, the wilderness is a period of frustrated grumbling and the forty years are a punishment for Israel's lack of trust in God. However, it is also the best time of their lives with God.

Listen to what the prophet Jeremiah says:

> The word of the Lord came to me: "Go and proclaim in the hearing of Jerusalem:
>
> > "This is what the Lord says:
> >
> > "'I remember the devotion of your youth,
> >> how as a bride you loved me
> > and followed me through the wilderness,
> >> through a land not sown.
> > Israel was holy to the Lord,
> >> the firstfruits of his harvest;
> > all who devoured her were held guilty,
> >> and disaster overtook them,'"
> >
> > declares the Lord. (Jer 2:1-3)

Israel is the Lord's bride. The wilderness is where they love the Lord best, like a young couple on their honeymoon. Israel's unfaithfulness to the LORD in the time of Jeremiah is compared to a bride who has forgotten her groom, forgotten her wedding. In chasing after other gods, Israel is like a woman chasing after other men. Yet, when God calls them to remember the Lord, their groom, they are called to recall the wilderness. The wilderness is a time of devotion, a time of love, a time of faithful following.

Which is it? Is the wilderness a time of grumbling or intimacy? Is it a place where Israel endures punishment and suffering or is it a place where they know God's presence, love, and provision? The answer is that it is both.

Two different stories are told of Israel's time in the wilderness: "One is driven by a sense of banishment, characterized by mistrust, expressed as quarrelsomeness, and devoted to return to Egypt. The other is the history of hope, trusting in

Yahweh's promises, enduring in the face of want and need, sure that history was on its way to the new and good land."[12] In Scripture, God gives us both stories and holds them both up as true. The wilderness is intimacy and rebellion, grumbling and growing in love.

What about our periods in the wilderness? How do we remember those times when we were uprooted from a comfortable place and entered into a time in the dry heat? How do we remember when all our coping mechanisms were taken away and all we had left was God?

For many of us, our wilderness times are that same mixture of pain, struggle, and closeness to God. Imagine living for years with chronic hip pain. When the pain is removed, it is glorious *and* a bit disorienting. We have lived so long with the pain that we learned to compensate for it. How we sat, how we moved, and how we slept were all affected by our pain. The removal of the pain is a blessing, but it also requires relearning so much. We need to relearn how to walk without adjusting to avoid the pain. We have been walking for years, but we need to relearn that basic function in order to live *without* pain, just as we learned to walk differently *with* pain.

When God brings Israel out of Egypt, he releases them from their bondage and pain. They have just spent four hundred years learning to walk like Egyptians. Learning to walk without the yoke of Pharaoh will take time, so God brings them into the wilderness. He draws close to them so that they can learn to walk again. "For you have delivered my soul from death and my feet from falling so that I can walk before God in the light of life" (Ps 56:13).

Relearning to walk before God instead of before Pharaoh is glorious, but comes with growing pains. Israel's grumbling, murmuring, and whining in the wilderness is the process of Israel coming closer to God and having all the ways of Egypt stripped away from them. For centuries, all their meat, bread, and fullness have come from the land of Egypt. For forty years, God gives them manna and quail to retrain them to look for life and sustenance from God. They had lived depending upon Pharaoh, but are now learning to depend upon God.

Leaving our Egypts can be a bit like dying, too. "This is the death that beckons us in the wilderness. It is a preparatory kind of brokenness that makes the heart ready for God's deeper work."[13] The ways we have grown accustomed to living, the coping mechanisms we have used to make it through life, and the crutches with which we have propped ourselves up are removed. We must relearn what it looks like to live. We might want the intimacy of the wilderness without the struggle, but God does not promise that.

Chuck DeGroat says that "Those early pages of the Exodus story disturb me because I want it to be easier... But the story of redemption, which is really the whole story of the Scriptures, is an excruciatingly long, tumultuous narrative full of resistance, battle, defeat, exile, reunion, and rebellion — stretched out over centuries. Couldn't it be simpler somehow?"[14]

The wilderness is both a place of struggle and intimacy. But the wilderness is where Israel goes once they get out of Egypt, in order to get the Egypt out of them. Repeatedly, Moses stands before Pharaoh and proclaims that the people must leave so that they can go and worship God. This is exactly what they do when they leave Egypt. The people are led to the foot of the mountain, into the presence of God. The wilderness is where Israel first meets God as *their* God, where they behold him in glory on Sinai. The wilderness is not an easy path for any of us, but it is where we meet with God.

JESUS IN THE WILDERNESS

If the wilderness is a place of struggle, rebellion, and ultimately meeting with the holy presence of God, it should come as no surprise that the wilderness also plays an important role in the life and ministry of Jesus Christ. Michael Horton claims that the whole of Jesus' life takes place, in one sense, in the wilderness. "The incarnation, obedience, and death of Christ take place in the "desert" of human rebellion, not in the promised land of consummated rest."[15]

By taking on flesh, Jesus enters the wilderness — he goes into a place of human grumbling and rebellion in order to be the holy presence of God with the people. The people of Israel have the presence of God among them in the tabernacle, which is situated at the center of the camp. In Jesus, the Son took on flesh and dwelt among us (John 1:14). We no longer have the tent of God in the wilderness — we have Jesus Christ in the tent of the flesh, dwelling in the midst of the wilderness of the world. He is God meeting with his people, drawing near and dwelling in our midst, so that we will not only be led out of the Egypt of sin and death, but will also learn to walk before God in the light of life.

It is not an accident that Jesus' first public act after baptism is to spend forty days in the wilderness (Mt 4:1). Jesus is the true Israel and his life follows the same path as Israel. Israel was baptized in the Red Sea (1 Cor 10:2) and then spent forty years in the wilderness. They grumbled, rebelled, and often disobeyed the voice of God. Jesus is baptized and then spends a period of forty days in the wilderness. He, too, faces temptations in the wilderness, but instead of succumbing to them, he stands firm upon the word of God. Jesus keeps what Israel broke. He fulfills what we do not.

Jesus has already walked ahead of us into the wilderness. We are not called to walk anywhere our Savior has not already walked. As God uprooted Israel from being rooted in Egypt, God also uproots us from our familiar bondage to sin and death. God sets us free and calls us to leave some things behind. He calls us into the wilderness, where our old ways of life will be burned away to make way for a life of intimacy with God. This painful wilderness path is how God led his people from being rooted in Egypt to being rooted in the promised land. We need to be rooted, as well, but rooted in life in Christ, rather than in the deadly land of sin.

The wilderness was a route on the way to the promised land. It was the path on which God took his people, so that they could leave behind the bondage of Egypt and embrace the freedom of the living Lord.

The journey to rootedness in Christ involves a similar movement. We are led out of Egypt in order to be led into the promised land. But in between, we walk through the wilderness. We are saved from sin and death and promised eternal life with Christ in the new heavens and new earth. But in between, we walk in the wilderness. As much as stability is part of the biblical calling of God's people, so is movement. We are constantly called to move out from patterns of sin into deeper union with Christ and holiness. We have been set free by the finished work of Christ. The Spirit continues to apply this salvation freedom to every area of our lives, calling us out of our Egypts into the wilderness. Yet ours is always a pilgrim theology. We are always people on the way to the promised land — we are always wilderness people. No matter how deeply rooted we become in our particular places and neighborhoods and no matter how good this stability is for our calling in this world, the wilderness is not our home.

Nonetheless, the wilderness is still where we draw near to God. Perhaps more accurately, it is where God draws near to us in love. This wilderness journey is the place where God loves us and claims us as his own. It is where we walk with

Jesus, traveling along the wilderness path he has already trod. This is where God carries us on eagles' wings and brings us to himself (Ex 19:4). This is the honeymoon, where the bride of Christ — the church — is led by God into the wilderness, experiencing his tender love and awaiting the day when it will be brought fully into his house.

"Not all who wander are lost,"[16] as Tolkien once observed. Israel's first experience of being a rooted people needed to end. They were rooted in Egypt and trapped in slavery. Being rooted is good, but being rooted in the wrong place can be deadly.

Whether it is the ancient Pharaoh or our modern-day pharaohs, the familiar security of Egypt leads to slavery and death. God broke Pharaoh's power over Israel in Egypt and called them out in the wilderness. That true freedom meant not only freedom from bondage, but freedom for service to God. This twofold freedom was seen in the crossing of the Red Sea and Israel's time at the foot of Mount Sinai. This twofold freedom finds its fulfillment in the freedom from sin and for life with God in Jesus Christ.

The wilderness was a difficult land, but Israel was never lost there. They struggled there, but were close to God. They wandered in the wilderness, but were led day and night by the presence of God. The wilderness was an important part of the journey from Egypt to Canaan, because through it, God weaned them from dependence upon Egypt and taught them to walk with him.

We, too, must often go through the wilderness in order to leave behind the bondage of sin and enter into deeper intimacy with God. Living rooted requires that we leave the comfortable, landed life in Egypt for the fragile, dependent life in the wilderness. The stability and rootedness of Egypt leads only to slavery and death; to find stability, we may need to be uprooted and led into the wilderness.

God uproots us from Egypt to lead us to the promised land. Yet, God also uproots us from the land in order to plant us in difficult soil, including the soil of Babylon.

7

GOD'S SCATTERED PEOPLE

KEEPING FAITH IN DIGITAL BABYLON

It can be hard to tell the difference between an exodus and an exile, especially when you're in the middle of one.
- Alastair Roberts & Andrew Wilson

Faith is precisely for exiles who remember the land but see no way to it.
- Walter Brueggemann

Contemporary life is filled with an almost constant stream of distractions and interruptions. As I write, my daughter needs me to get her something to drink. My son wants to tell me about his new project at school. My wife has her audio drama playing as she makes dinner. Life in a full house has always come with a certain amount of noise and activity.

However, even without interruptions, we are quite capable of distracting ourselves. I can only speak for myself, but this is often what my daily life looks like. A profound thought pops into my head that I *have* to tweet. I work a couple of minutes, then make the excuse to google something.

Five minutes later, I forget why I am on my phone, as I scroll through Instagram and like the pictures from everyone's vacation. I shake myself and try to get focused again. Two minutes later, I impulsively check Twitter to see if anyone has noticed (and liked) my tweet. My attention slips so easily as my phone buzzes. Even when no notifications come, I can find myself losing minutes at a time.

I have found that I am not alone.

The story of God's people did not end with them entering the land. Israel was taken out of the land and entered Babylon, yet they were not the only ones to enter exile. The rapid shift into the digital age has pushed the contemporary church into Digital Babylon. This age of distraction and instant gratification forms our souls in ways that make faithful discipleship difficult. This is the land of our exile and, like Israel before us, we must learn how to walk faithfully with our Lord *here*.

In this chapter, we will look first at Israel's exile from the land and the challenges they face in Babylon. We will then explore the particular pressures of the digital age upon our time, attention, and focus — pressures which create barriers for considering the gospel and living in light of it. Lastly, in a world with similar challenges and temptations as our ancestors faced, we will see the value of resilience in order to become rooted in Christ in this rootless land.

PEOPLE IN A FOREIGN LAND

As we have seen, God planted the people, he also eventually uprooted them. The history of Israel in Canaan was a slow spiral into forgetfulness. The prophets warned the people about the consequences of forgetting God. Yet, the people presumed upon God's promises. They said, in effect, "God promised that the land would be an *everlasting* inheritance, that he would be our God *forever*. God promised *this* place to

us. Surely, if judgment comes, it will fall on the wicked nations
— on *them*. Surely it will not fall upon God's people. Surely it
could *never* mean we would be uprooted from the land."

The prophets cried with increasing urgency, proclaiming
the message of the LORD: if the people did not return to God,
they would be ripped out of the land. First the northern
kingdom fell and was taken away by the Assyrians. Though
there were periods of revival, the southern kingdom of Judah
also descended into disobedience and idolatry. The kings there
promoted injustice, the people worshipped false gods, and the
land was filled with the stench of wickedness. As the end drew
near and the Babylonian army (sent by the Lord) surrounded
Jerusalem, the prophet Jeremiah prophesied the fall of the city:

> People from many nations will pass by this city and ask one
> another, 'Why has the LORD done such a thing to this great
> city?' And the answer will be: 'Because they have forsaken
> the covenant of the LORD their God and have worshiped
> and served other gods.'"
>
>> Do not weep for the dead king or mourn his loss;
>> Rather, weep bitterly for him who is exiled,
>> Because he will never return
>> Nor see his native land again. (Jer 22:8-10)

The people are sent into exile. Jerusalem falls, the temple is
torn down, and the people God planted in the land are
forcibly uprooted and carted off to Babylon. God gave them
the land and God can (and does) take it away. Just as in Eden,
the people cannot live in the land of promise while rejecting
God. For seventy years, they live cut off from the land. Nonetheless, God promises to bring them back.

The exile creates a crisis of faith. The temple, the center of
Israelite worship, is gone. How can their sin be removed
without the temple and the sacrifices? Yet the LORD promises,

""In those days, at that time," declares the Lord, "search will be made for Israel's guilt, but there will be none, and for the sins of Judah, but none will be found, for I will forgive the remnant I spare."" (Jer 50:20). Though the people cannot not deal with their own sin, God promises to forgive.

But what about the land? Will they be in exile forever? "This is what the LORD says: "When seventy years are completed for Babylon, I will come to you and fulfill my good promise to bring you back to this place"" (Jer 29:10). Like Israel in Egypt, the LORD will come to his people trapped in Babylon and lead them out into the land. Though the exile is a punishment for sin, God will bring about a new exodus to restore them to the land. "The prophets keep calling Israel to remember the exodus — but not in nostalgia for a golden age and certainly not in lament for tragedy, but in hope for the future."[1] On the other side of exile, God promises a new exodus, where he will lead the people out and renew his covenant with his people. ""This is the covenant I will make with the people of Israel after that time," declares the LORD. "I will put my law in their minds and write it on their hearts. I will be their God and they will be my people"" (Jer 31:33).

The problem of the exile is not merely with geography, but also with the soul. Israel's estrangement from the land mirrors their estrangement from God. The exile is not simply a time-out Israel receives for disobedience, so that, afterward, things can return to normal. The problem is that Israel has already uprooted itself from life with God. They have already left — choosing idols over God, choosing their own way over God's way. The exile, as painful as it may be, is physical reality coming to match spiritual reality. "Judah's problem, we discover, is deeper than physical captivity and harder to crack than mere armies. They are captive to sin itself: their iniquity, their faithlessness, their tendency to revert to idolatry even after they have been rescued again and again."[2] The new exodus on the far side of exile will require not only a restoration of place, but a renovation of the heart.

Yet, in the period of exile, in those years cut off and outside the land, what does it look like to be rooted in God? How do we live as God's people in a foreign land? Can we live faithfully in Babylon? From the Tower of Babel to the final pages of Revelation, Babylon is considered to be *the* place where people oppose God. "The Babylon of the Bible is characterized as a culture set against the purposes of God — a human society that glories in pride, power, prestige, and pleasure."[3] How can we live as God's people *there*? These are the questions faced by the likes of Esther and Daniel.

Like Joseph before them, Esther and Daniel are brought close into the halls of power. Unfortunately, this only leaves them more vulnerable. Their position comes with the possibility of influence for the protection of their people, but it also comes with temptation and peril. A wicked court official, Haman, plots to have the Jews exterminated (like Pharaoh before him, and far too many after him). Esther's cousin, Mordecai, becomes aware of the plot and informs Esther. Though she has become queen, Esther can only make an appeal for her people through subterfuge, and at great personal risk. She tells Mordecai, "Go, gather together all the Jews who are in Susa, and fast for me. Do not eat or drink for three days, night or day. I and my attendants will fast as you do. When this is done, I will go to the king, even though it is against the law. And if I perish, I perish" (Es 4:16). It is only God's providential work that protects Esther and the people.

Uprooted in Babylon, the people of God are vulnerable to the machinations of the powerful. The powers of Babylon will not tolerate competition. Daniel, Shadrach, Meshach, and Abednego are all elevated and then cast down because of their unwillingness to compromise their faith in the face of Babylonian pressure. Refusing to pray to the king or bow down to his statue, they are cast into fire and into the lion's den. Only the miraculous work of God rescues them from certain death. Babylon is a place where the people of God can die at any moment, where the pressure to compromise for the sake of survival is strong, and where only the gracious hand of God can sustain his church.

After seventy years in exile, the people are allowed to return to the land. However, only a small remnant actually go back. Most stay in Babylon or become scattered throughout the empire and across the Mediterranean. Even when they return, though, God's people are scattered. They are foreigners in a foreign land.

The return to the land is not, however, a return to things as they were before. The Israelites must adapt to and live in a new normal. Israel is no longer an independent nation, but has become a vassal state, first under one power and then another. The people can worship God (even rebuild the temple), but they are also pressured to do so according to the rules of the empire under which they live. Even back in the land, life is precarious. Even back in the land, the people still live in exile, still scattered awaiting God's redemption.

LIVING IN DIGITAL BABYLON

Babylon is not dead, it just went online. In their book *Faith for Exiles*, David Kinnaman and Mark Matlock describe our current culture in the West as "Digital Babylon." We, too, live in exile. Once Christian faith sat at the center of many communities — like Jerusalem sat in the middle of Israel. Now, that faith feels pushed to the margins. Many of us may have grown up near a "spiritual Jerusalem," but we now live in Babylon. Though we may not feel as if *we* have changed, the culture has certainly changed around us and it can be disorienting, particularly as change seems to occur faster and faster.

We sense that fewer people are religious (or at least believe in the same way). We have now moved into Babylon. No one asked us if we wanted to move, but we are there nonetheless.

> Ancient Babylon was the pagan-but-spiritual, hyper-stimu-lated, multicultural, imperial crossroads that became the unwilling home of Judean exiles, including the prophet Daniel, in the sixth century BCE. But *digital* Babylon is not a physical place. It is the pagan-but-spiritual, hyper stimu-lated, multicultural, imperial crossroads that is the virtual home of every person with Wi-Fi, a data plan, or — for most of us — both.[4]

While Ancient Babylon used the threat of physical violence to impose its will, Digital Babylon's weapons are more subtle, though no less powerful. The goal is not merely military conquest, but cultural conquest. As James K. A. Smith says, "Victoria's secret is that she is actually after your heart."[5]

Digital Babylon does not need swords and arrows to conquer us when it can use the internet and our smartphones. Whenever we consume content on the internet, whether through apps, videos, music, TV shows, or social media, we are being discipled. We are being shaped to consider some things important by how much attention they take from us. In this way, we can participate in our own colonization by Digital Babylon. "The idea of digital colonization may seem extreme, but here is the point: screens inform and connect, but they also distract and entertain. Through screens' ubiqui-tous presence, [Digital] Babylon's pride, power, prestige, and pleasure colonize our hearts and minds."[6] Digital Babylon works its way into our hearts through the devices we cannot ever seem to leave behind.

In short, our screens disciple us. Until we reckon with the

power of our screens, we will not be able to fully comprehend what it means to be living in Digital Babylon. Screens give us more information, but not more wisdom. According to research published in *Faith for Exiles*, the typical fifteen-to-twenty-three-year-old uses screen media 2,767 hours per year, but spends only 153 hours involved with spiritual content (of any variety).[7] Our screens have become the dominant way we engage the world and they shape us, whether we are aware of it or not. Why have a hard (and potentially awkward) conversation with our parents when we can simply look up the information on our phone? Anything we want to know we can learn in an instant. We have a wealth of information at our fingertips at all times. This ease of access to information offers great benefit in many areas of life, but it does not produce wisdom.

One of the great challenges of Digital Babylon is that we have increased our sources of information, while simultaneously cutting ourselves off from many sources of wisdom. In the words of Dr. Martin Luther King Jr., "We have allowed our technology to outdistance our theology and for this reason we find ourselves caught up with many problems."[8]

Our screens teach us to expect instant results. They unconsciously train us to be impatient with the seconds it takes to load a video — what about the months and years it takes to develop meaningful relationships? Patience and perseverance dwindle as we live in a world of instant gratification.

Furthermore, with the increased pace of technological change, we no longer look to the wisdom of previous generations to understand how to traverse this strange land. Instead of looking back for wisdom, we look next to us or in front of us. We look to friends or to algorithms to know how to handle this immense power in our hands. This cuts us off from significant sources of wisdom.

In a digital age, though, the church remains one of the few

places left in society where multiple generations come together, where sixteen-year-olds and sixty-year-olds sit side by side. Boomers and millennials may fight online, but they often sit next to each other in the pews on Sunday. They are brothers and sisters in the body of Christ. This shared life is a mutual source of *wisdom* in a world full of *information*.

FEAR OF MISSING OUT IN DIGITAL BABYLON

Digital Babylon also makes an idol out of fitting in and being "up to speed." "Screens promise more connectedness, but… loneliness, depression, and anxiety among teens have risen alongside widespread adoption of the smartphone."[9] We keep scrolling through Facebook, Instagram, or Twitter, just in case we missed something that is trending. We lament that a friend is not on social media, because we have no other way of connecting with them. We worry that they are constantly 'missing out' or being missed. Yet, this FOMO (fear of missing out) leaves many of us with a constant, crippling anxiety that someone, somewhere is having a great time without us. Despite our great connectedness online, we often experience a void of belonging. We can connect with like-minded people in many ways, but we have the deep sense that this connection is not quite solid. We fear that, for all our online presence, we are missing out on something real.

Life in Digital Babylon also shapes both how and whether we share our faith. Interestingly, digital technology can make it both easier and harder to share our faith with others. We have access to more biblical content on the internet than we have ever had before (particularly with so many churches increasing resources during the pandemic). Additionally, all it takes is the click of the button to share all that information — now, all 386 of my followers can read that article, watch that video, or check out that meme.

However, even though technology can make it easier to share our faith, it can also make it more difficult. Studies show that six out of ten millennials are more careful about how and when they share their faith because of digital technology. A similar percentage of millennials believe people will see them as offensive if they try to share their faith. Even more say they find themselves more likely than not to avoid real spiritual conversations.[10] In Digital Babylon, it may take only a few clicks to share a meme about Jesus, but it is becoming increasingly difficult to find a place where you can actually talk about him. The skepticism of our age makes it difficult to speak the truth of the gospel.

Additionally, in Digital Babylon, *everything* is considered crucial and newsworthy. To complicate matters, what counts as crucial changes rapidly. Each day brings a new topic of debate, a new news item, or a new crisis that we absolutely *have* to engage. We need to have an opinion about everything. If we lack an opinion on something, we must not care — a cardinal sin in the digital age of outrage.

Yet, while technology provides us with a greater awareness of our world than ever before, it also flattens everything to the same level of importance. "The space between the trivial and the crucial has shrunk. Everything is important all of the time, and you are obligated to keep up. Just as it is harder for us to sort all our correspondence when it comes to the same medium, it can be difficult for us to communicate the gospel if we primarily use mediums that are traditionally devoted to triviality."[11] When we see everything as crucial, we suddenly become unable to determine what actually matters and is worth our time. "Everything is crucial" also creates barriers to hearing the good news. When everything is (and must be) cranked up to eleven, we become numb to actual good news. We have difficulty recognizing the gospel when our brains and hearts are overstimulated by the constant clamoring for our attention. When confronted with something truly crucial, we are like the villagers who heard the young boy cry wolf too many times: we hear the words, but we let them pass over us.

THE SOUL-CRUSHING NATURE OF DISTRACTION

Digital Babylon is driven by distraction. Our most precious commodity in the digital age is not our time or money, but our attention. Boredom is the new enemy and everything we own is seeking to capture our limited attention. It might be convenient for my phone to remind me when I have set a dentist appointment, but it also reminds me I haven't been on Twitter in two hours, that I should really come back and play Candy Crush, and that the Detroit Tigers are playing and I am not watching. As soon as I finally settle in and get focused on work, my phone buzzes or an email alert dings and, by reflex, I have to check it. I don't even think about it. I grab my phone, and suddenly a few minutes disappear, and it takes another ten to fifteen minutes to get back focused on work.

The endless barrage of buzzes, dings, and notifications are all intended to grab our attention. Employers are recognizing the problem this creates in the workplace. Michael Hyatt, in his book *Free To Focus*, says, "Information is no longer scarce. But attention is. In fact, in a world where information is freely available, focus becomes one of the most valuable commodities in the workplace. But for most of us, work is the hardest place to find it. The truth is we live and labor in the Distraction Economy."[12]

As a leader and entrepreneur, Hyatt is primarily concerned with the loss of productivity in the workplace. "The cost of all this misspent time and talent is staggering. Depending on the studies you consult, the total time lost per day for office workers is three hours or more—as many as six."[13] Emails, meetings, drop-in visits, texts, calls, and notifications all create conditions where our days are drowned in busy work, but no real work gets done.

The problem of distraction, however, runs much deeper than the temptation to scroll through Facebook at work. Our inability to sit quietly with our own souls also creates the most significant spiritual problem of our times. When our hearts begin to ache, we self-medicate through technology. The discomfort, the quiet prick of our conscience, the unease that all is not right with ourselves, or even the hint that there might be something more — these fears are quieted quickly by watching another episode on Netflix, joining another Twitter crusade, or scrolling TikTok.

Alan Noble notes a truth that encompasses far more than himself, "Self-avoidance is probably my most advanced skill set...I'm always being encouraged to read something, to do something, to watch something, or to buy something new. It's an unspoken but mutually agreed upon truth for modern people that being alone with our thoughts is disturbing."[14]

Big questions take time to consider. It takes attention to examine our deeply held convictions, to wrestle with uncomfortable and potentially life-altering truths. Yet, utterly exhausted from needing to constantly know the *latest* thing, we have little energy to consider the *deeper* things. Trained to distract ourselves at the slightest sense of internal discomfort, we stop the hard work of soul searching before it even begins. "The problem occurs when antipathy toward sustained introspection and soul searching, cultivated through habitual distraction, becomes a barrier for hearing the gospel."[15]

The distraction at the heart of Digital Babylon is dangerous, not just for workplace productivity, but also for our souls. Through digital addiction, we numb ourselves to the prick of our conscience, an instrument the Holy Spirit uses for our redemption and sanctification. We sooth our conscience, not through confession and absolution, but through the rush of distraction. "When we've fooled ourselves into thinking we're at home with distraction, tricked ourselves into feeling "settled" only because we've sold our home-hunger for entertainment, then the irruption of the uncanny, a sense of not-at-home-ness, becomes a gift that creates an opening to once again face the question of who we are."[16]

For many of us, growing rooted in Christ may mean rooting out our distractions, so we can again face the question of who we are in Christ.

RESILIENT FAITH

Let's be honest — we are all in Digital Babylon now. We cannot go back to Jerusalem, at least not yet. We are called to live and to learn to live in this land of exile. We must, like Israel before us, learn to live as strangers in a strange land, to live as faithful people on foreign soil.

Digital Babylon shapes our hearts to desire a different kingdom than the kingdom of God. I am not arguing that technology is inherently bad and that all digital technology should be eliminated from our lives. Instead, we need to recognize *where* we live, we need to recognize the culture in which we live, and we need to recognize how that culture shapes us to love and value certain things. We have seen how Digital Babylon uses distraction and immediate gratification, giving us a way to self-medicate to avoid the most pressing questions of life and faith. If we are unaware of how our culture shapes us, we will be unprepared for the struggles our culture causes. "If we assume that for the most part society will continue down the path of adopting invasive and distracting technologies, the question facing Christians becomes not only how can we resist these changes but also how can we speak the truth in a culture where this is the norm?"[17] Like all exiles, we will need to learn specific patterns of resistance.

To survive in the barren and tempting land of Digital Babylon, we will not be able to rely on the roots we had in the land of Israel. Digital Babylon shows both the importance and insufficiency of being rooted in place. A stable commitment to a community and place offers one form of resistance to the pressures of Digital Babylon, as a way to live as exiles in a world committed to keeping up with the times and increasing the pace of life. "Stability as the revolutionary tactic of exiles is a gift from Israel's story to those of us who practice our faith amid the fragments of tradition in a world indelibly marked by mobility."[18] In a mobile, fast-paced world, the slow, patient work of remaining committed is a form of resistance.

Yet, staying in one place is not enough. Simply avoiding technological change or "slowing down life" is not enough. "The practice of stability can so easily become a strategy for resisting change."[19] What we claim as faithfulness can be a mask for stubborn commitment to the way things used to be. Simply being in the land did not solve Israel's spiritual crisis and it cannot solve ours, either.

We need to be rooted in something deeper — in Christ himself. Only when we abide in Christ, when we belong — not to ourselves, but to Jesus — will we be able to withstand the pressures of Digital Babylon. As we learned at the beginning of this journey, a little dryness causes the roots to run deeper. Digital Babylon is certainly a dry place. But these deep roots only lead to life if we are rooted in the right place, in Jesus Christ.

Digital Babylon may seem like a hopeless place to live. Yet, there are green shoots growing up amidst the rubble. In *Faith for Exiles*, Kinnaman and Matlock focus, not on identifying all that is wrong with Digital Babylon, but what is going right with resilient disciples of Jesus in these difficult conditions. They identify five key practices of resilient faith: intimacy with Jesus; cultural discernment; meaningful, intergenerational relationships; vocational discipleship; and countercultural mission.[20] While overlapping in many ways with *Faith for Exiles*, Part 3 of this book will explore particular habits in the life of the church that foster deeper rootedness in Christ in a rootless land. In particular, we will see how these practices — baptism, the Christian funeral, prayer and singing, the Lord's Supper, and growing in wisdom — arise from and intersect with the biblical story of God's people.

However, before we turn to practice, we need to return to the biblical story. We need to hear one more story to gain a full understanding of what land and exile mean for the people of God. We need to join God's people as they are scattered for mission.

8

THE MESSINESS OF MISSION

OPPORTUNITY AND CONFLICT OUTSIDE THE LAND

The Christian mission took its form from the Israel-centered world of the Old Testament and, equally importantly, from the inseparability, both historical and eschatological, of Israel's destiny from that of the nations among whom Israel was placed by God and throughout whom Israel had been scattered by God.

- Richard Bauckham

The call never comes when it is convenient. In five years as a firefighter, I never had my pager go off when it was a great time to put out a fire. It was always right before a meeting, in the middle of the night, or as I sat down to dinner. I tried to remember that, though this was bad timing for me, it was much worse for whoever had to call the fire department. Whenever the call came, however, I put down my knife and fork (or rolled out of bed), slipped on my shoes, and raced to the fire station.

When do we get called to mission? When we are in the land or in exile? Is it when the church is firmly rooted in place, or when we are scattered to the four winds? The answer is both. The call from God rarely comes when we think it is convenient. In the land, Israel is called to live for God in such a way that outsiders would be drawn in to worship the Lord. Yet, in the wilds of exile, God's scattered people are also called to live faithfully and to bear witness to God's character before the world.

The call never comes when it is convenient, but it does come, even — perhaps especially — in exile. By looking at the double movement of mission in scripture (drawing in and going out), we will see how the exile is not only a place of loss, but also a place of opportunity for God's people. For God uses his scattered people as the message of the gospel goes forth. The same lessons and challenges Israel faces in the exile exist alongside the call to mission. Conflict follows the church, even as conversions do. Despite how messy mission can become, we are called to share the good news that can draw together all the broken parts of our fractured age.

MOVEMENT ONE: DRAWING IN

Movement is part of the mission. From the days of Abram, God has called his people out of lands and into others. This call to move, to leave, to go, is tied to the mission God gives his people. God's call to Abram to "Go from your country, your people and your father's household to the land I will show you" (Gen 12:1) is followed immediately by God's promise: "I will make you into a great nation, and I will bless you; I will make your name great, and you will be a blessing. I will bless those who bless you, and whoever curses you I will curse; and all peoples on earth will be blessed through you" (Gen 12:2-3). God promises to make Abram a blessing to the nations. He promises to make something of Abram (a nation), but promises to do so for a purpose (as a blessing to nations).

When God calls his people out of Egypt, breaking the power of Pharaoh, and leading them out into the wilderness, God gives them a promise. "You yourselves have seen what I did to Egypt, and how I carried you on eagles' wings and brought you to myself. Now if you obey me fully and keep my covenant, then out of all nations you will be my treasured possession. Although the whole earth is mine, you will be for me a kingdom of priests and a holy nation" (Ex 19:4-6). God calls them to leave, then promises to make something of them. By their obedience and life before God, they let the world know what God is like. A holy nation and royal priesthood, Israel is set apart from the nations to live as a witness to the character and goodness of God.

Movement is part of the mission. The whole earth belongs to the Lord, yet he calls one people out of the mass of nations to be his own. By their witness to God, they are to draw the nations to worship and to serve the Lord. The goal of God's mission is not simply Israel itself, but the ends of the earth.

For much of the Old Testament, the movement of mission is *drawing in* those who are outside. Israel is a city on a hill, a holy nation, and its true, good, and beautiful life according to God's will draws the people of the nations to God. God includes provisions in the Law to address when foreigners want to start living like Israel (Lev 17:8-16) or want to eat the Passover (Ex 12:48), because the assumption is that this will happen. We are even told that when Israel leaves Egypt, many Egyptians go with them (Ex 12:38), drawn not by the holiness of Israel, but by the holiness and power of God.

Drawing in the nations is also part of the visions given to Isaiah:

> In the last days the mountain of the LORD's temple will be established as the highest of the mountains; it will be exalted above the hills, and all nations will stream to it. Many

peoples will come and say, 'Come, let us go up to the mountain of the LORD, to the temple of the God of Jacob. He
will teach us his ways, so that we may walk in his paths.' The
law will go out from Zion, the word of the LORD from
Jerusalem. (Isa 2:2-3)

The image is Israel at the center of the world, with the
nations streaming to Mount Zion to enter the temple of God
in worship. "Implicitly in the Old Testament it is Israel that is
pictured as the centre of the inhabited world and the nations
most distant from Palestine are placed at the edges of the
world."[1] God places Israel at the center to draw those on the
edges into the light of his presence.

In some ways, God did place Israel at the center of the
world. The land of Israel sat at the crossroads of the major
empires of its day, giving Israel incredible opportunity to
witness to the world of the goodness of God. "Israel's story is
certainly not one of parochial isolation, and it is indeed Israel's
geographical location, what Ezekiel calls her centrality among
the nations, that makes it clear that her destiny is bound up
with that of the nations: her immediate neighbors, the great
empires to whose power she succumbs, and even the more
distant nations whom those empires bring into Israel's view
and occasionally into actual contact with Israel."[2] Israel was
strategically placed so that the Israelites would not be an
isolated people in the wilderness, but a people called to be holy
along the trade routes of life and in the midst of empires. Israel
was called out of the nations to be placed at the center so that
God would use them to draw all people to himself.

MOVEMENT TWO: GOING OUT

The dominant movement of mission throughout much of the
Old Testament is God drawing outsiders in. However, there

are hints of a second movement that will become much clearer in the time of the New Testament. Isaiah not only sees the nations streaming to Mount Zion, but speaks also of God's law going forth from Jerusalem (Isa 2:3). There is a *drawing in* and a *sending out*. Most prophets prophesied to the nations from within the land of Israel. However, Jonah is sent out to Nineveh, to bring them the word of the Lord and to call Nineveh to repentance. Richard Bauckham notes that in the Bible there are "Two directions of movement: the centripetal and the centrifugal...moving in to Jerusalem or out from Jerusalem."[3]

This double movement — moving in and moving out — helps reframe God scattering his people in the exile. The exile itself is God's judgment. The prophets persistently proclaim that the exile results from the people's unfaithfulness to God. They are uprooted from the land and scattered to the corners of the earth. At the end of the period of exile, some of the people return to the land. We have the stories of Ezra and Nehemiah that speak of the struggles to rebuild the temple and walls of Jerusalem after they have been torn down. Some people are called back to the land to bear witness to the goodness of God in the midst of the world, to worship and to draw others to move in to Jerusalem. However, most of Israel remains outside of the land. Many people do not come back, but remain scattered in the cities of Egypt, Babylon, Greece, and later Rome.

The Diaspora — the time when the people of God live outside the land — is a significant loss. Many buckle under the pressure to conform to the patterns and idols of other nations. Many forget their distinctive identity and calling as God's people. They are like the prodigal son who goes to the far country and ends up longing to fill his stomach with the food the pigs are eating (Lk 15:13-16).

Many others, however, take a different path. They gather together around God's word, form synagogues, and educate themselves and their children in the Word of God. They live in close-knit communities, which help strengthen them as they strive to live for God in a hostile culture. In short, instead of returning to the land, they become rooted in God in other lands. They set up new centers where God can draw people to worship and serve him. Instead of being centered around the temple in Jerusalem, they now gather around the Word in the synagogue. Where once there had been one people, one land, one center, there are now suddenly hundreds of communities. In every major city, there is a Jewish community seeking to live faithfully in the midst of the culture. By rooting themselves in God's Word, even outside the soil of Israel, the people of God continue to participate in God's mission.

This is the world into which the Son takes on flesh as the man, Jesus Christ. The people of God are both gathered and scattered. The temple has been rebuilt and many people have returned to the land of Israel, seeking to live faithfully to God in the land he has given them. Yet, many others remain rooted in the scattered lands where God put them. Jesus' ministry takes place predominantly in the land of Israel, but its goal is, nonetheless, still the ends of the earth.

After his resurrection, Jesus appears to his disciples for a period of forty days. At the end of those forty days, Jesus is prepared to ascend to his rightful place at the right hand of the Father. He first asks the disciples to wait in Jerusalem, but then tells them, "But you will receive power when the Spirit comes on you; and you will be my witnesses in Jerusalem, and in all Judea and Samaria, and to the ends of the earth" (Acts 1:8). Once the waiting is over, once the Spirit comes, the movement happens. The disciples are sent out to be witnesses of the resurrected Jesus. Whereas, before, the movement of drawing people in was in the foreground, the movement of sending God's people out into the world now takes center stage.

The early twentieth century German theologian, Emil Brunner, made this observation about the church: "The Church exists by mission, just as a fire exists by burning. Where there is no mission, there is no Church."[4] To be the church is to be in mission – to be caught up in the mission of Jesus Christ by the power of the Spirit. We don't have 'missional churches' and 'non-missional churches': we simply have the church.

The community the Spirit called has been called to participate in the great and glorious mission of God. That mission involves movement. It involves going out into the world in order that outsiders may be drawn in to the people of God. God sends out his people to Jerusalem, Judea, Samaria, and to the ends of the earth.

OPPORTUNITY

This means that the scattering of God's people is a place of opportunity. Paul and the other early Christians are sent out into a Roman empire that already has little pockets of leaven mixed into the dough of the surrounding culture. There are hundreds of small faithful communities of God's people waiting for the coming of the Messiah. This is why, in almost every city, Paul goes first to the synagogue. Because there is already a community in each city of the empire that should be eager and ready to hear that God's promises have been fulfilled in Jesus, he starts by sharing the good news with the scattered people of God. By scattering them, God has helped put in place the conditions that will allow the gospel to spread to the four corners of the earth.

For the gospel to spread, the Jerusalem church must be scattered. After generations of thinking that God's mission is primarily to draw others in, the people must have found it hard to shift to intentionally going out to the world. The early Jerusalem church grows mightily, but remains centered very closely in Jerusalem. When problems arise regarding the caring for widows, a group is appointed to oversee their care, including a man named Stephen. "Now Stephen, a man full of God's grace and power, performed great wonders and signs among the people. Opposition arose, however, from members of the Synagogue of the Freedmen (as it was called) — Jews of Cyrene and Alexandria as well as the provinces of Cilicia and Asia — who began to argue with Stephen. But they could not stand up against the wisdom the Spirit gave him as he spoke" (Acts 6:8-10).

Eventually, Stephen is accused on false charges and brought before the leaders. He delivers a powerful speech proclaiming Jesus and accusing the Jewish leaders of resisting the Holy Spirit. At this, he is condemned to death by the rage of those listening. They drag him from the city and stone him to death. Stephen is the first martyr for the name of Jesus.

After the death of Stephen, the church is pushed into greater mission, almost against its will. "On that day a great persecution broke out against the church in Jerusalem, and all except the apostles were scattered throughout Judea and Samaria" (Acts 8:1). The people leave the comfort of Jerusalem and enter the countryside. Though fears of persecution likely make them anxious, something interesting happens: "Those who had been scattered preached the word wherever they went" (Acts 8:4). They may have been scattered by persecution, but they have been scattered carrying the message of Jesus. Even as they go to Judea and Samaria, the gospel goes with them. Remembering Jesus' promise in Acts 1:8, the apostles and later believers are witnesses in Jerusalem. Now they have been pushed to be witnesses in Judea and Samaria as well. The mission of Jesus continues.

Though persecution is not good in itself, God uses it to get his people moving on mission. Just as the exile was a judgment that God used to put his people where they needed to be across the known world, God uses even the evils of persecution to lead his people toward the ends of God's gospel mission. "Luke's account of the movement of the gospel from Jerusalem outward depicts a literal diaspora of the Jerusalem church, driven by persecution from Jerusalem, some as far as Antioch, where the Gentile mission first began in earnest."[5]

Paul, who had once led the persecution of the church, is turned around by God and sent out as a missionary. He and his companions work tirelessly to see the gospel reach all the way to the ends of the earth. Much of the book of Acts details Paul's various missionary journeys and the churches he plants, and concludes with Paul arriving in Rome, the figurative "ends of the earth." "Missionary progress in the second half of Acts is a continued exodus cycle. Believers are forever leaving cities — often where they have been suffering — before venturing off into foreign lands, flourishing and succeeding, incorporating Gentiles in their number, and returning in triumph."[6]

Everywhere Paul goes, God's people are already there. Antioch, Philippi, Corinth, Ephesus, Galatia, and even Rome already have small communities of faith when Paul arrives. The people scattered through exile have become rooted in these new lands. Paul, traveling the Roman roads, can anticipate a community of God around every corner. Sometimes, they receive him and the message he brings. Sometimes, they do not. Still, the presence of the scattered people creates opportunity for mission.

We can look at the scattering of the people in much the same way we understand Jesus' parable of the soil. Israel was scattered like seed from the hand of God. They were thrown by exile to the four corners of the land. Some withered and died in exile, abandoning the faith. Some struggled under the pressures of the world around them. Yet, some seeds managed to burrow deep into the soil and grow.

In pockets around the empire, there were seeds of Israel that grew in new soil, ripe and ready for harvest. Thus, when Paul and others travelled throughout the empire, they found a harvest everywhere they went. They also scattered seeds among the Gentiles and found the Spirit working powerfully in those communities as well, but they went first to scattered Israel to find a harvest of faith in Jesus. As Jesus himself promised, "The harvest is plentiful, but the workers are few. Ask the Lord of the harvest, therefore, to send out workers into his harvest field. Go! I am sending you out like lambs among wolves" (Lk 10:2-3). When Paul and others went out in the field, they found the harvest ready.

We can look at our rootless, scattered, mobile world as both a loss and an opportunity. We have already looked at all the ills and pains that come from rootlessness: a loss of iden-tity, insecurity, struggles to love our neighbor, hidden vices, loneliness, anxiety, and much more. Clearly, rootlessness creates many of the ills of our age, and, unfortunately, it seems to be growing rapidly in our culture.

Yet, we must also recognize that the very rootlessness we see creates an incredible opportunity in our world. As megachurches crumble and large Christian institutions wane, we may find ourselves increasingly in a similar situation to the world of the New Testament, where small, marginalized churches sought to live a life of faith in a hostile world. Yet, these very circumstances were so fruitful for mission in the early Church. These small pockets of people living out their faith in local communities were not a loss, but a gain. Paul could come into a town, proclaim the good news, plant a church, and then leave in a relatively short time because there was already a community established with the maturity and relationships necessary to foster the ongoing growth of the church.

The scattering of the church in the West can offer a similar opportunity. We can relearn the second movement of mission. Though God gathers his people, he also sends us out to be his witnesses. Though Christians rightly gather in corporate worship, the people of God no longer need to find their center in the temple in Jerusalem, but in the person of Jesus Christ. "This new centre is everywhere and nowhere, just as with the advent of modern geography and postmodern globalization the ends of the earth are everywhere and nowhere."[7]

In New Testament mission, people are not drawn to a particular place, but to a particular person: Jesus Christ.[8] The gospel proclamation draws people not into the Holy Land but to the Holy One. While physical place and space are important, the dislocation of the church in the West can force us to remember where our roots truly lie. They lie not in the land, but in the Lord. Like Israel scattered before us, we can learn to live as God's people where he has scattered us. This is an opportunity to engage in mission, not to rue the loss of status for the church. "The church in the west may have to get used to the idea that its own centre in God, from which it goes out to others in proclamation and compassion, is actually a position of social and cultural exile or marginality."[9]

CONFLICT

Though there is incredible growth on those first missionary journeys, there are also weeds mixed among the wheat. Though many in the synagogues hear the good news and rejoice, others also resist. Paul's most vicious opponents are frequently those who should be most eager to listen (Acts 17:5-15, 18:5-6, 18:12, 19:8-9). Resistance and hatred often come from within the synagogues. Frequently, those who should be leading the charge of faith instead lead mobs that drive the apostles out of town.

The church also experiences hatred and violence from civil authorities. The apostles, accused of inciting the wrath of the gods and treason, are whipped, beaten, and imprisoned by the Roman authorities for disturbing the peace. Paul goes before local governmental leaders many times and eventually appeals all the way to the Emperor. The church sees an abundant harvest from both Jews and Gentiles, but also experiences abundant hatred.

The scattering of God's people among the nations leads to significant conflict. Some are drawn in by the Spirit of God, but others are repulsed. The presence of the church and the proclamation of the gospel lead to a twin response. "To the one we are an aroma that brings death; to the other, an aroma that brings life. And who is equal to such a task?" (2 Cor 2:16).

Just as many come to faith and are drawn to worship and follow Jesus, the world's hatred is also stirred up. When those who had become disciples were happily following the ways of this world and walking in sin, there was no resistance from the world around them. They were going with the flow of the world (even if it was against the way of God). Yet, once they turn around (the literal translation of the word 'repent') and start swimming in a different direction, the believers face all kinds of resistance. When they walk according to the ways of God, rather than the ways of the world, their lives become harder, not easier.

The lessons learned living in exile are also necessary for living in mission. The resilience, patience, and endurance required to live in exile are also essential to live in mission, even when the harvest is plentiful. In fact, the church in the New Testament is described as a community of exiles. In Peter's first letter, he begins this way: "Peter, an apostle of Jesus Christ, to those who are elect exiles of the Dispersion in Pontus, Galatia, Cappadocia, Asia, and Bithynia" (1 Pet 1:1). He refers to the church as "elect exiles," that is, those who are chosen by God even as they are not at home in the world.

That Peter refers to the people as elect exiles demonstrates the twin realities of Christian identity. As Christians, we are "elect," or chosen. We are defined first by our relationship with God — we are chosen in him. This relationship with God also creates a particular relationship with the world — we live here, but never truly belong here. We are "exiles" in this world.

Like others living in exile, we may put down some roots, but we always have a sense that this is not our true home. We are able to live in any land and in any culture, because we live everywhere as exiles. This is true regardless of where we find ourselves. There is no land and no country where we will not find our heavenly citizenship creating conflict. No land or country is our true home. Our true home is in heaven, where Jesus is.

Living in exile requires, to some degree, being in a consistent space of discomfort, with a sense that we never truly belong. We may do many of the same things and participate in many of the same activities as everyone else in our communities. We may go to the store, buy homes, get married, educate our children, and even pay taxes, but we do them in different ways or for different reasons. Like God said to Israel as they went into exile, Christians are able to "Build houses and settle down; plant gardens and eat what they produce. Marry and have sons and daughters; find wives for your sons and give your daughters in marriage, so that they too may have sons and daughters. Increase in number there; do not decrease. Also, seek the peace and prosperity of the city to which I have carried you into exile. Pray to the Lord for it, because if it prospers, you too will prosper."

(Jer 29:5-7). We genuinely live in the lands where God has put us.

However, at other times, we will be unable to participate in what the world is doing, or will participate in markedly different things, with different values, ends, and means than the world around us. "Beloved, I urge you as sojourners and exiles to abstain from the passions of the flesh, which wage war against your soul" (1 Pet 2:11). Christians are called to live by the law of the land of their true citizenship. That means that, whether we live in a republic, democracy, or monarchy, we live according to the will of our King, Jesus.

As Peter tells us, when we make the world our true home, we follow the passions of the flesh. We see this particularly today in how our culture views our passions. We are our bodies, we are our desires. To "be ourselves" is to follow our desires, because our desires are perceived to be the core of who we truly are. To deny our desires, or to suggest that we should deny ourselves anything we want, is an attack on our very selves, on our sense of identity, on our humanity. This explains why Christian ethics, particularly sexual ethics, induces so much rage today. Because of this false understanding of humanity and what it means to be human, the world views Christian insistence on "abstaining from the passions of the flesh" as violent oppression.

When we live according to God's Word, we see that, while humans *have* desires, we *are not* our desires. Our desires can be denied for the sake of a greater good, can be redirected toward a better end, or can even be deferred to a more appropriate time. We are truly free because we are not slaves to our passions — because we know that the center of our identity is belonging to Jesus Christ. Our desires are part of who we are, but never lie at the center; instead, they serve the center — Jesus Christ. This is an example of when Christians must live and behave as "elect exiles." We must expect that, in a world where "you are what you desire," the Christian call to abstain from certain passions will be met with disdain and resistance.

What are these passions of the flesh from which we are called to abstain? "The acts of the flesh are obvious: sexual immorality, impurity and debauchery; idolatry and witchcraft; hatred, discord, jealousy, fits of rage, selfish ambition, dissensions, factions and envy; drunkenness, orgies, and the like. I warn you, as I did before, that those who live like this will not inherit the kingdom of God." (Gal 5:19-21).

How, instead, are we to live as those who belong to the true King? "But the fruit of the Spirit is love, joy, peace, forbearance, kindness, goodness, faithfulness, gentleness and self-control. Against such things there is no law. Those who belong to Christ Jesus have crucified the flesh with its passions and desires. Since we live by the Spirit, let us keep in step with the Spirit. Let us not become conceited, provoking and envying each other." (Gal 5:22-26).

Christian conviction and practice create conflict. The same message that saves is the one that inflames. Some will rejoice and repent, while others will reject the message and kill the messenger. The same dual reaction that we see in the New Testament is the lot of the church in our own culture.

There is great opportunity in our mobile, scattered culture. The message of the gospel is a balm for those feeling the fracture of our age. The gospel first went forth in an age like the one in which we live. The seeds of the gospel first took root in small communities surrounded by a hostile culture. Everywhere the gospel went, conflict followed. The apostles were both received and rejected, welcomed into some homes, but driven out of many towns. The same may be true of the church today.

The mission of the church involves movement. Outsiders are drawn in to worship and to praise the living God. God's people go out to share God's Word. We see this pattern throughout the Bible. Though there was more emphasis on "drawing in" in the Old Testament and more on "going out" in the New, both are present throughout the Scriptures. The church needs both movements in a culture that is both aching for the good news of the gospel, but nonetheless resistant to it.

As Christians, we can be tempted to prioritize one type of movement over the other. We see this when we set up a false competition between worship and mission. Some believe that what we really need to revitalize the church is better worship, more holiness, or better programs — if our gathered life and worship is good, true, and beautiful, then the church will be renewed and people will come to follow Jesus. Others argue that what we really need is to go out and evangelize, to serve, to do justice, love mercy, and walk humbly with our God out in the world.

No, we need to gather people in.

No, we need to go out to the world.

This is a false competition. God gathers and scatters his people. Aside from the fact that many of these arguments make the growth of God's kingdom about our work and not the Spirit's (a significant problem), the most important thing to understand is that *both movements are in Scripture*. We are sent out in order to draw people in. God gathers and scatters his people. He did it with Israel and does it with us. Thus, there is no competition between going out in service and gathering in worship, between doing justice and praising the only one who is worthy, between evangelism and discipleship. As the two movements belong together in Scripture, so they belong together in the life of the church.

Being able to put off the passions of the flesh and cultivate the fruit of the Spirit will not happen through our effort. It will not be a result of some magical pill or even the most well-conceived plan. Instead, it will come when we trust the Spirit to work through deep habits to root us into our identity in Christ. In the messy context of mission, we need now — more than ever — to find ourselves rooted and abiding in Christ. It is to this need that we turn in part 3 of this book.

ABIDING IN CHRIST

Abide in me as I abide in you.
Just as the branch cannot bear fruit by itself
unless it abides in the vine,
neither can you unless you abide in me
John 15:4 NRSV

9

CUT OFF AND BROUGHT IN

CIRCUMCISION AND BAPTISM

How long will this last? How do you find relief from this kind of crushing loneliness?
  - Wesley Hill

By it [baptism] we are received into God's church and set apart from all other people and alien religions, that we may wholly belong to him whose mark and sign we bear.
  - Belgic Confession, Article 34

I remember stepping down into the large baptismal pool, robed in white. I remember how warm the water was. I remember looking up and seeing my family, friends, and mentors gathered around me. I remember the mixture of peace and panic as the minister placed a cloth over my face before plunging me into the water. "I baptize you in the name of the Father, and of the Son, and of the Holy Spirit. Amen." I remember coming up from the water, wet and washed, joy upon my face.

When I remember my baptism, I remember a moment. Yet, more than that, I remember a reality, a promise, a claim

God made upon my life, even if I did not fully understand it at the time. "I am not my own, but belong — body and soul, in life and in death — to my faithful savior, Jesus Christ."[1] God did something on that day and I will spend the rest of my life living differently because of it.

Some Christians can remember the moment of their baptism. They remember the sights, touches, and sounds. Other Christians, though, have no recollection of being baptized. They were baptized as infants, before they could utter a word. Both those who remember and those who don't were marked by God. Both received his promises in baptism. Both were called to faith and faithfulness in response to God's claim upon them.

Whether we remember the moment or not, it is the reality of baptism, not our memory of it, that makes us rooted in God's covenant people. God's promises, signified and sealed in the waters of baptism, root us in Jesus Christ. We live and move and act because we *already* belong — not in order to belong. Because Jesus lived and died for us, we can now, in gratitude, live and die for him. Remembering our baptism — the reality, not necessarily the moment — is a key component for living rooted in Jesus Christ.

Baptism is a gift that roots us in our identity in Christ and our relationship with God. In order to understand this gift, we need to look at the deep relationship between circumcision and baptism. Baptism and circumcision cut us off from our old self and bring us into fellowship with God and his people. In this chapter, we will look at the institution of circumcision in Genesis 17, including the mark of circumcision itself and who was marked with it. Then we will wrestle with circumcision as a mark of being cut off when loneliness and isolation already run rampant in our world. Finally, we will see circumcision's fulfillment in baptism and how God cuts us off from sin in order to bring us into relationship with Jesus.

CUT OFF IN CIRCUMCISION

God's people experience being cut off. God calls Abram to leave his country, land, and family (Gen 12:1). Abram leaves them all behind to follow the LORD. Abraham's descendants — heirs of the promises and the covenant of God — are also called to be cut off. They are to be separate, different from the nations, holy. God gives them a distinct way to dress, a distinct calendar, distinct foods, and distinct rituals. He gives them a distinct way of life, loving God and loving neighbor. In all these ways and more, God sets his people apart. They are cut off because they belong to God.

In the ministry of Jesus, this cutting off is heightened. Jesus tells us that following him will cut us off from mothers and brothers (Lk 14:26). He promises to divide families (Lk 12:53), something Christians throughout the centuries have felt only too well. Coming to faith in Jesus, particularly when our family has not, often means being cut off in one way or another. Faith in Jesus can divide families even as it brings us together into the family of the church.

In Genesis 17, God's command to be cut off as a sign of belonging to him takes physical form. Circumcision is removing some of the skin around the head of the penis, known as the foreskin. God chooses circumcision as the mark of membership in this covenant relationship. To belong to God, to receive the blessing of relationship with him, Abraham and his people must all be circumcised.

Circumcision is a surprising mark of the covenant between God and his people because it is not visible to the world. Later, on Mount Sinai, God's people are given particular ways to eat, dress, and act that set them apart from the people around them. Yet, this most fundamental mark of belonging to God — circumcision — is not readily visible to others, but is instead largely hidden. A covenantal relationship with God, then, becomes visible not through some easily seen mark, but through a life transformed by relationship with God.

Circumcision is painful and bloody. In circumcision, part of you is cut off and removed in order to be in relationship with God. This physical mark, though, is a sign of a deeper cutting. Those who belong to God are not only to be cut in the flesh, but cut to the heart. The prophet Jeremiah describes this as a circumcision of the heart (Jeremiah 4:4). Their hearts were to be cut by the covenant so they could live in communion with God.

Just as physical circumcision is painful, so too is circumcision of the heart. The desire to live on our own must be cut off. The hunger to make a name for ourselves apart from God must be cut off. The desire to live in defiance of God must be cut off. All so that we can be in communion with God.

Circumcision is painful — a cutting off, a cutting away, a removal. It is a sign in the body of what will be done in the heart to mark one as belonging to God. It is also a gift. Apart from that circumcision, that cutting of the heart, we can easily live with all the external appearances of relationship with God, but our hearts are far from him.

Circumcision is also permanent. It doesn't wear off and it cannot be undone. As a permanent physical mark on the body, circumcision is a sign of the permanent nature of God's relationship with his people. As the LORD says, "My covenant in your flesh is to be an everlasting covenant" (Gen 17:13). As lasting and permanent as the sign of circumcision is in the body, so also is God's covenant with his people.

Lastly, circumcision is serious. It is not optional. "My covenant in your flesh is to be an everlasting covenant. Any uncircumcised male, who has not been circumcised in the flesh, will be cut off from his people, he has broken my covenant" (Gen 17:13-14). To refuse the mark of the covenant, to refuse circumcision, is to reject the heart of the covenant: relationship with God. The only options are to be cut through circumcision or be cut off from God and his people by rejecting circumcision. The mark of covenant membership is not optional.

WHO IS MARKED?

Who is marked by circumcision as belonging to this covenant, as being in relationship with God? Infants and Gentiles. Listen to this: "For the generations to come, every male among you who is eight days old must be circumcised, including those born in your household or bought with money from a foreigner — those who are not your offspring. Whether born in your household or bought with your money, they must be circumcised." (Gen 17:12-13).

The first group to undergo circumcision are eight-day-old infants. Circumcising infants is a highly counter-cultural practice. Circumcision was only practiced occasionally in the ancient world, usually for men who were about to become priests. Furthermore, those who were circumcised were always adults. The youngest a man would typically be circumcised would be at puberty.[2] But God instructs Abraham to circumcise children at eight days old.

Before the child can speak, before it can lift up its head, before it can even remember the circumcision taking place, the child is marked as belonging to God. Before the child can choose God, the child is already chosen. Before it can even begin to love God, the child is loved by God. Contrary to the common practice of the culture, God established circumcision not to mark a decision to devote oneself to God, but as God's act of claiming this child as his own.

The second group to undergo circumcision are outsiders. Specifically, God talks about those who were not physical descendants of Abraham. These are Gentiles, non-Jews. From the outset, God has in view that people who are not physical descendants of Abraham will be brought into the covenant. Outsiders, who were bought at a price, will be marked as belonging to God, as one of his people forever. Would these adults have made their own decision to be included and undergo circumcision? Yes, but circumcision is still God's gift, God's mark claiming this person as his own. We see in the covenant with Abraham that God has always intended his grace to extend to the nations. It has always been God's design that those who are outside will be invited in, those who are far off will be brought near, those who were once not God's people will become God's people.

CUT OFF IN THE PIT OF LONELINESS

In circumcision, God calls us to be cut off. Yet, many of us already feel cut off far too much of the time. Even before social isolation became a matter of public health, loneliness plagued Western culture. Though the COVID-19 pandemic has made this much worse, we were already dealing with a "Loneliness Epidemic."[3] Household size has been dwindling; more and more people live alone; the social structures that support healthy communal life are fraying or being replaced by digital substitutes. Nearly half of all Americans (almost double the rate in 1990) report having three or fewer close friends. Twelve percent report having no close friends at all, quadruple the rate in 1990.[4] Loneliness has reached the point that many governments are appointing officials to help combat it[5]. We already live painfully cut off from one another.

Some of this isolation is a result of the pervasive rootlessness we find in our culture. When appointing the world's first "Minister for Loneliness," British Prime Minister Theresa May reflected that, "For far too many people, loneliness is the sad reality of modern life."[6] We may have a thousand friends on Facebook and a blue check on Twitter, but still feel lonely more nights than not. We see picture after picture of people out enjoying life on Instagram while we load the dishwasher for the third time today. The relationships that help combat loneliness are harder to maintain with sufficient depth as people continue to move in and out of communities. Third spaces — that is, places other than home and work, where social interaction can happen and is nurtured — are dwindling. Our primary way of connecting is often online, which may give us an initial lift, but often makes the later crash much worse. If friendship and community are the meat and potatoes of social life, digital interactions are like sugar cubes. If they are our main diet, we are liable to get sick. As a culture, we can be more connected than ever, but more rootless as well.

However, some of the ache of loneliness can be present even in healthy communities. We groan, along with creation, for redemption, longing for union, living with the pain of separation from God, ourselves, and others. We feel profoundly cut off even in the midst of people.

In his books, *Washed & Waiting* and *Spiritual Friendship*, theologian Wesley Hill names the deep loneliness that marks us all in different ways. He tells of an Easter Sunday spent in worship, study, food, and genuine friendship. Yet, even in the midst of the day's joy, he found himself fighting despair. Even as he felt so loved and so close to others, he felt an aching loneliness churning in his stomach. Hill remarks, "How strange is it, I thought as I backed out of their driveway, that I just spent the whole day with people — some of whom I would count among my best friends in the world — at two Easter dinner parties and a Bible study, and I still feel so desperately, utterly, helplessly lonely?"[7]

We are made for life with God. Our hearts remain restless when we look anywhere else. Yet even when we seek to find our rest in God, some of the ache remains. Until Christ returns, we long for a union we have not yet received.

This unfulfilled longing and loneliness is not the sole purview of single people. Even within healthy marriages, we can feel loneliness, as we long for more intimacy. Hill tells of a friend who admits, "When I get home from work, it's great. My wife is there to greet me, and she always asks about my day...But the problem...is that then I'm wishing she'd ask *ten more questions*! I'm always wishing she were more curious about me. I'm always feeling like I want her to know me better." Even in relationships with so much closeness and intimacy, like marriage, we can find ourselves wanting more. We want more than others can give — more time, more love, more closeness — and it can leave us feeling cut off.

Loneliness, feeling cut off, is not necessarily being sad and forlorn all the time. It can also be the feeling of ache that comes alongside the joy. "Loneliness can make your life painfully contradictory. You can be on a roller-coaster high one day and in the depths of despair the next. Sometimes you can experience both on the same day. Sometimes in the same moment."[8] We can be so close to one another and yet ache with how far apart we truly are.

The current "epidemic of loneliness" has only heightened what we have lived with since departing Eden. We wonder if anyone will ever truly know us — not what we project to the world or even show to our friends, but the real person we are underneath. We fear the vulnerability necessary to show ourselves fully to someone else. What if they hurt us? What if they reject us? What if we find out we do not truly belong?

However, we also fear that if we were to give ourselves fully, it will be too much. People will not handle our full selves, with all that we are. So we cut ourselves off.

We are born for life with God and life in relationship with one another, but we are also born cut off because of our sin and the sinful world in which we live. Unfortunately, as we grow, many of us cut ourselves off even more, hiding ourselves from each other and God, pasting fig leaves to cover our shame. We find ourselves, like Bonhoeffer, wondering who we are: "Am I then really that which other men tell of? Or am I only what I myself know of myself?...Who am I? This or the Other? Am I one person today and tomorrow another?"[9] We can become cut off even from ourselves.

We already feel far too cut off far too much of the time. We live uprooted and cut off from the place God has set us. We live longing for connections and desperately hoping that something will end this ache of loneliness. We even live cut off from those closest to us and can feel cut off from ourselves. In this world east of Eden, why would the LORD tell us we must be cut off? Why would he place cutting off, circumcision, as the sign of being part of the covenant with him?

THE CIRCUMCISION OF JESUS

Jesus knows what it is like to be cut off. He undergoes circumcision eight days after he is born (Lk 2:21). He experiences the cutting off that marks him as part of the covenant people. Jesus also identifies and experiences the cutting off we know so well.

Down on the banks of the Jordan river, Jesus is baptized. Luke introduces him almost casually in this passage (Lk 3:15-22), as just one among the many others who have come to be baptized. But something is different. Even before the Spirit descends and the voice proclaims the identity of this man, something is different.

The baptism of John was a baptism of repentance, a proclamation from sinners that they will turn from their sin and walk with God. However, Jesus has no need to repent. As all of the Bible unanimously declares, Jesus has never sinned.

There is never a breach in his relationship with God caused by disobedience. Therefore, there is no need for Jesus to be baptized in the Jordan with the rest of these sinners.

But he is baptized in the Jordan. At the very outset of the ministry of God's anointed, he identifies with sinners. He declares his solidarity, his oneness with sinners by being baptized in the Jordan, even though he himself doesn't need to repent.

Already in his baptism, Jesus is the one who would take another's place, who would be covered in the water, who would be buried in another's place. Already, we get a glimpse of the Messiah who will come as the Savior of the world.

Jesus goes out into the wilderness, where he faces the wiles and temptations of the devil (Lk 4:1-13). He then returns to his home village, where he is run out of town (Lk 4:14-30). He gathers disciples and, though they listen to him and follow him, they do not understand him. They misunderstand his mission and his identity time and time again.

Jesus' whole life involves humiliation, not just on the cross. After the last supper, Jesus goes to Gethsemane to pray and the disciples fall asleep. Jesus is left alone, struggling in this hour of prayer. When Judas betrays him, the disciples flee, as Jesus predicted they would. Jesus faces the sham night trial, the mocking, spitting, beating, and whipping alone (Lk 22:63-71). He faces Herod Antipas and Pilate alone (Lk 23:1-16). Ultimately, he goes to the cross alone. His disciples gone, only John and the women gather at the foot of his cross (Mk 14:50, Mt 27:55-56, Jn 19:25-27).

Jesus' ministry is one of being cut off, his whole life is a form of circumcision. Throughout his life and chiefly in his death, Jesus is cut off for the sake of sinners. He enters the pit of loneliness, crying out in dereliction on the cross, in order that we might be brought into the people of God. Jesus' cutting off is not simply a move into isolation and loneliness, though; it also opens a way for us into fellowship with God.

If the only meaning of circumcision is a cutting off, it might lead us to despair. If we have only the pain of the cutting, we might wonder whether this is truly good news. Yet, we are cut off in order to be brought in. We are cut off from the world and from our sin so that we can be brought into the family of God, into relationship with God himself. On the far side of the agony of the cutting, we find the joy of the covenant. Our "cutting off" need not be an entry into isolation and loneliness; it can be an entrance into a new community, the church.

BROUGHT IN BY BAPTISM

The heart of the covenant in Genesis 17 is God giving himself in relationship to human beings. In the covenant of circumcision, we are cut off, but we are also brought into relationship with God.

> I will establish my covenant as an everlasting covenant between me and you and your descendants after you for the generations to come, to be your God and the God of your descendants after you. The whole land of Canaan, where you now reside as a foreigner, I will give as an everlasting possession to you and your descendants after you, and I will be their God. (Gen 17:7-8)

"I will be your God." That is an astounding claim. In this covenant, God promises himself to Abraham. The God of the universe, God Almighty, binds himself into relationship with human beings. God promises Abraham a people — children and descendants. God promises Abraham a place — the whole land of Canaan. God gives Abraham a place to belong and a

people to whom he can belong, both of which are important. God's greatest gift to Abraham, however, is God himself. He enters into a covenant, a marriage-like relationship, with Abraham and his descendants. God promises to keep his side of the covenant: a people, a place, and communion with God himself. God humbles himself in love to be Abraham's God, to be in a unique, intimate, special relationship with Abraham and his people. At the heart of the covenant, God promises himself to Abraham. Abraham has to keep his side of the covenant: circumcision.

As God promised, Abraham has children and descendants who become a nation, one that lives for four hundred years under bondage in Egypt. After God leads them out of that bondage, he brings them to the foot of a mountain, where He renews his promise that he will be their God and they will be his people.

Within days, however, the people show that while they have been circumcised in the flesh, many have not been circumcised in their hearts. They fall down and worship a statue of a golden calf, proclaiming it to be the god who brought them out of Egypt. Their bodies bear the mark of belonging to God, but their hearts are far from him. Yet, God does not give up on his promise to have communion with his people. Generation after generation, this pattern of being marked in the flesh, but hard in the heart, continues. Yet, God does not give up. Instead, he promises a new covenant, where what is written in the flesh through circumcision will be written on the hearts of God's people through the work of the Holy Spirit.

God promises a new covenant, where the Spirit will mark God's people and circumcise their hearts. God's covenant to be their God is an everlasting, unbreakable promise. Eventually, God himself comes as the man Jesus Christ, and on the night in which he is betrayed, he takes bread and breaks it and after supper he takes the cup and says, "This cup is the new covenant in my blood." (Lk 22:20). With the coming of Jesus comes the new covenant. Through his bloody and painful sacrifice, Jesus opens the way for us to feast with God. The joyful relationship that was promised is made visible at a table, in a meal.

Less than a day later, Jesus is crucified. Three days later he is raised from the dead. Fifty days later, as his disciples are gathered in the temple, the Spirit descends upon them in fire. Peter stands up and proclaims the good news of the Gospel:

> When the people heard this, they were cut to the heart and said to Peter and the other apostles, "Brothers, what shall we do?"
>
> Peter replied, "Repent and be baptized every one of you in the name of Jesus Christ for the forgiveness of your sins. And you will receive the gift of the Holy Spirit. The promise is for you and your children and for all who are far off — for all whom the LORD our God will call. (Acts 2:37-39)

At the word of the gospel, hearts are cut, circumcised. In response, they are told to be baptized. They are told that the promise of God — forgiveness and relationship with God — is for them, for their children, and for all who are far off.

What was Abraham told? The covenant was for him, his children, and those bought with a price — for infants and Gentiles. At Pentecost, the promise of God made all the way back in Genesis 17 is fulfilled by the giving of the spirit and the waters of baptism.

In the new covenant, baptism replaces circumcision as the sign of membership in the covenant. We no longer need to be circumcised to belong to God. Instead, we are brought to the waters of baptism.

Listen to Paul's word in Colossians: "In him you were also circumcised with a circumcision not performed with human hands. Your whole self ruled by the flesh was put off when you were circumcised by Christ, having been buried with him in baptism, in which you were also raised with him through your faith in the working of God, who raised him from the dead" (Col 2:11-12).

We no longer need to be circumcised by human hands in order to be in God's covenant people, to be in everlasting relationship with him. Instead, we must be baptized. Baptism replaces circumcision, but it is remarkably similar. It is not easily visible to the world, but should lead to a life transformed by relationship with God. While baptism does not involve a cutting off of our flesh, it does involve a cutting of our hearts through the work of the Spirit. Baptism, like circumcision, is permanent and does not wear off, and it is serious. Because of the deep connection between circumcision and baptism, it is also offered to infants and Gentiles. It is graciously given to children born in the household of God and adults who were once far off but have been brought near by the blood of Christ. Baptism is the mark of membership in the covenant, which explains why the church has always made baptism a prerequisite for coming to the Lord's Table, and why many churches place the baptismal font on the way to the table. We must first be washed and claimed in order to eat with God. We must first belong to God in order to feast in his presence. We must first be marked as his own to come close and join in the feast of the new covenant.

Baptism marks us as belonging to the family of God. It is not only a mark of being cut off from the world and from our sin, but it is also a mark of being brought into covenantal relationship with God.

The ache of loneliness will not truly go away until Christ returns. Yet, the Lord provides balm in baptism. By uniting us with Jesus Christ, we are cut off from the world and brought in to relationship with Jesus Christ. Loneliness may linger while this age lasts, but the gift of life with God and the gift of the community of the church are a comfort as we await those final days. "The remedy for loneliness — if there is such a thing this side of God's future — is to learn, over and over again, to do this: to feel God's keeping presence embodied in the human members of the community of faith, the church."[10]

When we are baptized, we belong to Jesus. We have our place in Jesus Christ. Our firm foundation stands. "God is our refuge and strength, a very present help in trouble. Therefore we will not fear, though the earth should change, though the mountains shake in the heart of the sea; though its water roar and foam, though the mountains tremble with its tumult" (Ps 46:1-3).

Living in a rootless world, living east of Eden, can feel like the earth is constantly shifting and trembling, like we can never find our footing. Yet, plunged beneath the waters, cut off from our old self, baptized into death, we are set high upon the rock. "For who is God except the LORD? And who is a rock besides our God? — The God who girded me with strength, and made my way safe. He made my feet like the feet of a deer, and set me secure on the heights" (Ps 18:31-33). When we emerge from the waters of baptism, we have been brought into a new community, the community of the Son.

In baptism, our isolation is ended. We may still feel lingering loneliness or the weight of sorrow in this day, but we have truly been brought into fellowship with God. We have been given our place in Him. We have been washed and given wedding garments and now we await the feast when the bridegroom will come. We have been cut off from the old life, the ways of sin, death, and the devil. Yet, we have been cut off so that we can be brought into communion with Jesus. Baptism is washing away the dirt and bringing us into the house.

Living rooted will mean remembering our baptism. Whether we remember the event or not, we cling to the free gift of our gracious entry into the covenant people. In baptism, we have been washed, cut off from our old life of sin. Christ promises that "as surely as water washes away the dirt from the body, so certainly his blood and his Spirit wash away my soul's impurity, that is, all my sins."[11] In baptism, we have been brought into covenant fellowship with God. In our world, we might deal with loneliness, worry we are too much, or feel cut off from those around us. Yet, we have been brought into true fellowship with the Triune God and Christ's bride, the church. Loneliness does not get the last word. Jesus does.

Remember your baptism.

10

BURIED IN HOPE

THE CHRISTIAN FUNERAL

Death is a mystery to us. Yet the Living One has passed away, passed through death, holding its keys.
  - J. Todd Billings

He drank the cup of suffering to the last drop and tasted death in all its bitterness in order to completely deliver us from the fear of death and death itself.
  - Herman Bavinck

When I pulled up to the nursing home, I did not know I would be seeing Shirlene for the last time. I had come with an elder to share the Lord's Supper with her. We came ready to share the Word and invite Shirlene to the feast of the Lord. As soon as we turned into her room, I knew something was different. Her grandson welcomed us into the room. Shirlene was tired. Hospice had been called, a sign that everyone in the family knew what she had already known. Death was approaching. We didn't know how soon, but it was coming.

The elder stood with her grandson while I knelt beside

Shirlene's bed. Her voice was weak and our conversation short. I shared Psalm 23, which includes a promise made all the more poignant in situations like these: "Even though I walk through the valley of the shadow of death, I fear no evil, for you are with me. Your rod and your staff, they comfort me" (23:4).

Then, in a few short words, I shared the gospel again with Shirlene. It was a story she had long known and which had long formed the center of her life. Noticing her weeping grandson, she turned toward him and told him, in a raspy voice, "I love Jesus very much, it is going to be okay." She did not say that it would not be hard to lose her. She did not say we should not cry or that death was not a tragedy. Yet, she was not afraid of death because she knew Jesus. She knew her savior, knew his love for her, trusted in his one sacrifice on the cross to redeem her, and believed she would be raised up and enter the presence of the Lord.

Shirlene knew what the Heidelberg Catechism proclaims, that our only comfort — in life and in death — is that "I am not my own, but belong — in body and soul, in life and in death — to my faithful savior Jesus Christ. He has fully paid for all my sins with his precious blood and has set me free from the tyranny of the devil. He also watches over me in such a way that not a hair can fall from my head without the will of my father in heaven. In fact, all things must work together for my salvation. Because I belong to him, Christ by his Holy Spirit ensures me of eternal life and makes me wholeheartedly willing and ready from now on to live for him."[1] Shirlene was rooted in Christ even in the face of death.

Each of us will die. The Christian faith invites us to neither minimize death nor be overwhelmed by it. Instead, we face it fully with the hope we have in Jesus. This utter confidence in God's promises enables us to remain rooted in him, even in those moments when life shakes us most violently, even when death comes. We see this same beautiful hope as Abraham buries his wife, Sarah, at Machpelah.

MOURNING AT MACHPELAH

Sarah's death is the first and only time that the span of a woman's life is given to us in the Bible and it is the first time we see death mourned in the Bible. "Sarah lived to be a hundred and twenty-seven years old. She died at Kiriath Arba (that is, Hebron) in the land of Canaan, and Abraham went to mourn for Sarah and to weep over her" (Gen 23:1-2).

Back in Genesis 5, we hear the genealogy of Adam all the way down to Noah. It goes something like this: So-and-so lived such-and-such amount of time and had a son, then lived so many more years, had other sons and daughters, and then he died. Nine times, all men, and 'then he died.' Interestingly, there is no mourning recorded for any of those deaths. It is as if, after being kicked out of the Garden, death just becomes normal. It is just a fact of life. We don't mourn the sun setting, or the winter coming, either. Death is just the way things work in this world.

Something changes with the death of Sarah. Abraham draws near to his dead wife Sarah and weeps over her body. Something changes. God has entered into covenant relationship with Abraham and now death is seen for what it is. It is wrong. It is the enemy. It is an affront to the way things should be. At the bedside of Sarah, something changes because God's covenant with Abraham heightens the stakes of life and death.

God draws closer to Abraham and Sarah and, in doing so, life becomes sweeter and death more bitter. Abraham and his offspring can no longer pretend that we live in a world where 'death is a door' or 'death is the next great adventure' or 'death is like the changing of the seasons.' Instead, we have heaven and hell, either everlasting joy or the eternal lake of fire.

God drawing near to Abraham reveals the heart of the biblical story — we are made for fellowship with God. Sin has ripped that away and death, the fruit of sin, cuts us off from the life God gave us. God's promise to Abraham of life, blessing, land, descendants, and relationship with God only raises the stakes for what is lost in death.

This explains why we, as Christians, of all people, can mourn. We do not mourn, though, as those without hope (1 Thess 4:13). We believe in the resurrection of the body and the life everlasting. We believe in the risen Jesus Christ who promises that all who are baptized into his death and believe in his name will be raised up on the last day. Yet, that hope can make our pain sharper so that, like Abraham, we sit and weep beside the bodies of those we love. Because we know the gift of life, we can see and feel the horror of what is taken in death.

When God draws close to Abraham, Abraham's mourning increases even as his joy increases. His relationship with God sharpens the pain of death even as it gives him hope that God will overcome it.

Abraham's mourning for Sarah is instructive for us. In our increasingly post-Christian world, we often find ourselves pushed to minimize our grief in the face of death. Isn't death just natural, a part of the life cycle? Isn't earth just a small speck in the galaxy and humanity just one species on the planet? What does one death matter in the scope of the universe?

In a world increasingly desensitized to the reality of death, where death has no face, but is simply a number on a stat sheet, we still know that death matters. Our Christian mourning for the dead is a radical witness to the value of life in a world that cheapens it. When we continue to gather at funerals and at bedsides to weep over those who have died, we proclaim that the life of *this* person is a gift from God. We mourn because death takes a life so valuable that the Son of

God went to the cross to die for it. When we mourn with Abraham, we proclaim with him the wrongness of death, even as we hold fast to the hope found in the resurrection of Jesus Christ.

HOPE IN THE FACE OF DEATH

The closer God draws to us, the sharper our hope and the sharper the pain of death often become. The nearness of God presses upon us the firm hope of the resurrection. "Therefore my heart is glad and my tongue rejoices; my body also will rest secure, because you will not abandon me to the realm of the dead, nor will you let your faithful one see decay" (Ps 16:9-10). God's faithfulness even in the grave, which is fulfilled in Jesus Christ (Acts 2:26-27), is for all who are united to Christ by faith.

> People, despite their wealth, do not endure;
> they are like the beasts that perish.
> This is the fate of those who trust in themselves,
> and of their followers, who approve their sayings.
> They are like sheep and are destined to die;
> death will be their shepherd
> (but the upright will prevail over them in the
>   morning).
> Their forms will decay in the grave, far from their
>   princely mansions.
> But God will redeem me from the realm of the dead;
> he will surely take me to himself (Ps 49:12-15).

Though death is the fate of all people, God's faithful love penetrates the grave. God stoops down to lift the poor from the dust and make them sit with princes (Ps 113:6-7). He also reaches down into the grave to raise up his children. As James

K. A. Smith says, "The hope of enduring love, a love stronger than death, is not some natural immortality; it is a life bought by the death of God, the resurrection of the Crucified, which now yields hope as a spoil of victory over the grave."[2]

> The cords of death entangled me,
> The anguish of the grave came over me;
> I was overcome by distress and sorrow.
> Then I called on the name of the LORD:
> "LORD, save me!"
> The LORD is gracious and righteous;
> Our God is full of compassion.
> The LORD protects the unwary;
> When I was brought low, he saved me.
> Return to your rest, my soul,
> For the LORD has been good to you.
> For you, LORD, have delivered me from death,
> My eyes from tears,
> My feet from stumbling,
> That I may walk before the LORD
> In the land of the living (Ps 116:3-9)

Whether from death itself or from all the death-like places in which we find ourselves in this life, God's presence heightens our hope because God promises to save. This hope echoes across the New Testament, the consistent comfort of Christians throughout the ages. "But Christ has indeed been raised from the dead, the first fruits of those who have fallen asleep. For since death came through a man, the resurrection of the dead comes also through a man. For as in Adam all die, so in Christ all will be made alive. But each in turn: Christ, the first fruits; then, when he comes, those who belong to him" (1 Cor 15:20-23).

When the perishable has been clothed with the imperishable, and the mortal with immortality, then the saying that is written will come true: "Death has been swallowed up in victory." "Where, O death, is your victory? Where, O death, is your sting?" The sting of death is sin, and the power of sin is the law. But thanks be to God! He gives us the victory through our Lord Jesus Christ (1 Cor 15:54-57).

To live and die in the Lord Jesus is to live and die in the comfort, confidence, and hope of the gospel. "For to me, to live is Christ and to die is gain" (Phil 1:21). However, to be cut off from God is to be cut off from this hope.

Speaking of their lives before they were in Christ, Paul says to the church in Ephesus, "remember that at that time you were separate from Christ, excluded from citizenship in Israel and foreigners to the covenants of the promise, without hope and without God in the world" (Eph 2:12). Apart from Christ, death retains its tragic character only. The victory Christ has won over death is shared only by those who share in Christ. The conquest of death in Christ is a victory for those who are *in Christ* by the Spirit. Apart from Christ, death swallows and consumes and leaves only despair. "Let us eat and drink, for tomorrow we die." (1 Cor 15:32, citing Isa 22:13). Yet in Christ, death is swallowed and consumed by Christ's resurrected life. In Christ, there is life and hope even in the face of death. For this reason, Christians can experience death as a place of hope, as a staging point for resurrection.

DEATH IS NEVER JUST A NUMBER

The closer God draws to us, though, the sharper the pain of death. Our hope grows, but so does our sense of loss. Gripped by the full value of life, we also feel the full horror of death. We often seek to minimize our fear of death by making it normal, almost not worthy of thought or consideration. Constant reports of death tolls scrolling across the bottom of the screen remove the faces from death. They join the baseball scores as just another statistic, another fact without real impact on our lives.

During the pandemic, newscasters have often tried to portray the severity of the crisis by listing ever larger numbers of infections and deaths. However, for many, these growing numbers have not had the effect the newscasters intended. After years of seeing deaths as numbers on the screen, we have become numb to the numbers. Like a weird reversal of Abraham's plea for Sodom, we begin to wonder how many people need to die before we should get worked up. Five? Ten? Fifty? A hundred? A thousand? The problem becomes not the numbers themselves, but the fact that they have become *just* numbers to us. Years with death ever-present in the news and yet always distant have trained us to live with a certain detachment toward death. It is real and ever-present and yet *not* real at the same time.

James K. A. Smith accurately describes our contemporary attitude toward death. "Death is deferred — to others, to "later." When it comes to death *in general*, we are certain that everyone dies. But when it comes to our own death, Heidegger says, we are "fugitives" from the truth: we run from facing it."[3] This distinction between 'death in general' and our own death reveals why many people responded very differently to the pandemic once a close family member (or they themselves) contracted COVID-19. Until that point, it was something 'out there,' something that happened to 'other people.' Death was a statistic until it became personal.

Christian faith should lead us deeper into the pain of death. Death is never just a number, never simply a statistic on a screen. In Genesis 5, we get a list of names, ages, and deaths that reads like a news report, but, in the death of Sarah, we are confronted with the full weight of death. She is someone made in the image of God, a beloved member of the covenant people, and she is dead.

Alan Noble points out our cultural resistance to mourning. "Our culture treats mourning as a mental health problem to be overcome...The loss of a human life is not just an *event* that causes a psychological *consequence*. The mourning we experience reflects the reality that each human life is significant and made in the image of God."[4] We are made to live life before the face of God, in deep, abiding communion with God. Death breaks this life.

Death both removes someone made in God's image and ends a life made to live with God. Rather than reducing or minimizing death, Christian faith forces us to confront it. We understand death as a profound loss. As Noble says, "The sense that life as we know it should stop when a loved one dies is, I believe, one of these prototypical human experiences...We have two primary ways to interpret the feeling: either it is a profound frustration caused by the absurdity of imposing meaning on an indifferent and meaningless world, or perhaps it is a reflection of the deeper reality that each human life is in truth just that significant."[5] We mourn because human life is just that significant. Drawing closer to God, and thus closer to the truth of life and death, will sharpen the pain of death, even as it rests us firmly on the soil of hope.

THE CHRISTIAN FUNERAL

Grief and hope sit side-by-side in the Christian funeral. One does not obliterate the other in the service, even if the final note of hope rings more strongly. We live our faith when we come to bury our dead.

In my own tradition, the Christian Burial is a service centered on scripture and prayer, proclaiming both our lament and our trust in the God of resurrection. It is a "service of witness to the resurrection." A statement of purpose, early in the service, captures the unique characteristics of a Christian funeral and illustrates how holding grief and hope together is a witness to life in Christ in the midst of a rootless world. It goes like this:

> We are gathered here to praise God,
> to witness to our faith,
> and to give thanks for the life
> of our *sister/brother N*_____.
>
> We come together in grief,
> acknowledging our loss.
> May God grant us grace
> that in pain—we may find comfort,
> in sorrow—hope,
> and in death—resurrection.
> Dying, Christ destroyed our death.
> Rising, Christ restores our life.
> In baptism, *N*_____ was sealed by the Holy Spirit
> and marked as Christ's own forever.[6]

This statement (and thus the whole service) connects death with baptism. The burial completes the dying that began in baptism. It is an act of resurrection hope that God will keep the promises made in baptism ("For you Jesus Christ came into the world; for you he died and for you he conquered death")[7]. Additionally, this statement of purpose holds out both the reality of grief and loss ('we come together in grief, acknowledging our loss') and the firm hope of the resurrection ('dying, Christ destroyed our death. Rising, Christ restores our life').

For Christians, attending a funeral can be an act of resurrection hope. For most people, funerals are something we only attend when a family member or close friend dies. Yet, Christian funerals are for the whole church. They are a chance for the whole body of Christ to walk these last steps of the journey of faith with a brother or sister in Christ. They are also a chance for the church to recall her resurrection hope in Jesus Christ. The funeral is both a burial of the dead and a witness to the living of the hope for those who belong — body and soul, in life and in death — to our faithful savior, Jesus Christ.

We live in a world where everyone we will ever love will die one day. The ever-present pressure of death leads some in our world to withdraw from love, to seek to avoid the pain with a pattern of self-protection. However, rather than causing us to pull back in the face of death, the Christian faith, according to James K. A. Smith, calls us to lean into loving others:

> The solution to loving mortals isn't to withhold our love in a protective hedge against loss; rather, we can love long and hard, trusting in the God who is all in all, who gathers up our losses in a time beyond time. Even our grieving is suffused with hope because all our loves are caught up in the immortal Beloved who loves us first. All is not lost.[8]

Because we know that Jesus Christ has entered death, has conquered death, and has promised resurrection for his own, we can stare death straight in the face, mourn deeply, and then keep on loving. Abraham mourns Sarah because there is genuine loss in her death. We, too, can face up to the real, deep loss that death causes in our lives. Christians are free to mourn deeper than others because we know the full value of life and the full horror of death. Yet, Christians can also be more hopeful in the face of death, because we trust in the God whose love is stronger than death.

MACHPELAH: DOWN PAYMENT ON THE PROMISE

Following Sarah's death, Abraham buys the cave at Machpelah. It is a place to bury the one he loves, but it is so much more. For Abraham, the cave of Machpelah represents so much more than a little piece of land. God has promised Abraham that his descendants will one day occupy the whole land of Canaan. The acquisition of Machpelah is a down payment on that promise.

At the time of Abraham, foreigners were not allowed to purchase land. Even today, as I learned during our journey to buy a house in Canada, being a foreigner makes purchasing property incredibly complicated. But, in the days of Abraham, it simply is not done. Foreigners are not allowed to buy land. Even though Abraham has been living in the land of Canaan for over fifty years, he is still a foreigner, still not one of them. So he asks if they will bend the rules and sell him some property so that he can bury Sarah.

Abraham repeatedly says that he wants to buy the land, making it clear that he does not want to borrow it. The Hittites, the people living in that land, try to find a way to help Abraham without selling him the land. First, they offer to let him use any of the best tombs in the land, free of charge. When Abraham asks to buy a specific piece of land for the full price, the owner tries to give it to him. Abraham insists, however, that he must buy it.

After Ephron the Hittite relents, Abraham weighs out 400 shekels of silver for the land. It is possible that Ephron exploited Abraham and overcharged him, but it is difficult to know with any certainty. Abraham pays the price and obtains the land.

The end of the chapter feels a bit like something we might find on the desk of a lawyer:

Abraham agreed to Ephron's terms and weighed out for him the price he had named in the hearing of the Hittites: four hundred shekels of silver, according to the weight current among the merchants. So Ephron's field at Machpelah near Mamre — both the field and the cave in it, and all the trees that are within the borders of the field — was deeded to Abraham as his property in the presence of all the Hittites who had come to the gate of the city. Afterward Abraham buried his wife Sarah in the cave in the field of Machpelah near Mamre (which is at Hebron) in the land of Canaan. So the field and the cave in it were deeded to Abraham by the Hittites as a burial site (Gen 23:16-20).

Abraham pays the price and receives the deed to the cave at Machpelah, as well as the field in front of it. This is the first time God's people take possession of a piece of the promised land. It is a down payment, a foretaste, the first fruits of the promise God made to Abraham. As Abraham approaches the end of his life, he gets a taste of the promise. He won't live to see Israel march across the Jordan, walk around Jericho, or conquer the land. He won't live to see his descendants sit under their own fig trees or worship in the temple of the LORD. He won't live to see the generations come to know the LORD in the land. He cannot imagine that the LORD himself will walk across this dusty ground as the man Jesus Christ. Abraham won't live to see all that, but as he purchases the cave at Machpelah and buries Sarah there, he gets a taste of what God will do.

Machpelah is a down payment on the promise of eternal life. As the first piece of the land to come into the possession of God's people, it serves as a promise that they will one day receive their inheritance.

The book of Hebrews makes the connection clear:

All these people were still living by faith when they died. They did not receive the things promised; they only saw them and welcomed them from a distance, admitting that there were foreigners and strangers on earth. People who say such things show that they are looking for a country of their own. If they had been thinking of the country they had left, they would have had opportunity to return. Instead, they were longing for a better country — a heavenly one. Therefore God is not ashamed to be called their God, for he has prepared a city for them (Heb 11:13-16).

Machpelah is not simply about the promise of the physical land of Israel, an earthly inheritance. The Patriarchs have their hopes set on a better country. Their hearts are set on heaven, where they will dwell in the presence of God. Even in the face of death, they hold fast to the hope of the resurrection. Speaking of Abraham offering Isaac on the mountain, the book of Hebrews says that "Abraham reasoned that God could even raise the dead, and so in a manner of speaking he did receive Isaac back from death" (Heb 11:19). Confident that God can raise the dead, Abraham purchases Machpelah and buries his wife, Sarah.

As a down payment, Machpelah is a place of both fulfillment and promise. It is where Abraham finally begins to have a place in the land and yet it is also a reminder of the promise to come. Christian burial is much the same. In this life, we already experience the beginnings of God's promises for us, but we still die and are buried in hope of that last day when Christ shall come. As at Machpelah, the promises of God are both a present reality and a future promise. As J. Todd Billings says, "God's promises *are* fulfilled in Christ, but God's kingdom *will* come in fullness in the future, when his reign is uncontested — until then, we lament, crying out with Revelation 22:20, "Come, Lord Jesus!""[9]

We already receive forgiveness, grace, and fellowship with Christ, but one day we will know the fullness of his embrace. We already have freedom from sin and life in Christ, but one day every tear will be wiped away and death will be no more. Death has already been swallowed up in victory, but one day death itself will be thrown into the lake of fire. Billings reminds us that Christians live experiencing God's faithful goodness now, nonetheless knowing there is yet more to come. "Those who trust in a God who promises already have promises that apply to the present, but they always live in hope."[10]

How we approach death shows our rootedness in Christ. In Christ, we feel both the full weight of death as a violation and tragic cutting off of the life of an image-bearer, but also as something that has been conquered in Jesus Christ. So how should we approach death? How should we face the reality that each of us will die, even in those moments when we feel farthest from death? As Christians, we should reflect on Machpelah and go to funerals. We should mourn and sing. We should weep and laugh. We should lift up our sorrow to the Lord and lift up our voices in praise for his faithfulness and his promises.

At Machpelah, Abraham mourns Sarah. Yet at Machpelah, Abraham receives a down payment on a future reality, a heavenly city. Death is a tragedy, but we are also buried in hope of the promised resurrection. Contemplation of the heavenly city can be a gift for living this side of Christ's return. As Michael Allen notes, the contemplation of heaven does not make us "no earthly good," but is an integral part of Christian spirituality.[11]

The Christian funeral is a practice that bears witness to and deepens our rootedness in Christ. Abraham buries Sarah in hope. He lays her to rest trusting God's promises. He weeps and his tears, as well as ours, bear witness to the pain of death even as we cling to God. In a world that often minimizes death by inundating us with it, Christians are called to face the full tragedy of death. However, we do not mourn without hope. The resurrection promise is for all who are in Christ. Thus, regularly attending Christian funerals can be a way for the church to contemplate our mortality, hold fast to Christ in the face of death, and recite the hope that is found in Jesus.

In his research on death and dying, J. Todd Billings discovered that different groups of people have wildly different responses to thinking about dying. "On the one hand, when young and middle-aged people encounter poignant images that make them reflect on their own death, they turn inward and go into survival mode, becoming aggressive toward those who hold different worldviews."[12] For many of those on the younger side of life, thinking about death closes them off to others. They become protective and defensive.

Billings notes, however, that "On the other hand, persons diagnosed with a terminal illness, persons who recover after nearly dying, and the elderly (who frequently reflect on their own death) do not have such a reaction. They do not turn inward in defensiveness. On the contrary, their sustained habit of reflecting on their own death opens them to others, even to those who are different from their "in-group"."[13] For one set of people, knowing they will die stokes fear and leads to isolation and animosity. For the other group, contemplation of death or dying enables them to turn outward to others.

These distinct responses follow all the different forms of rootlessness we have already explored. For some, the shaking ground causes them to circle the wagons, close ranks, and protect their own at all costs. For others, the quaking around them strips the barnacles from their lives and frees them to turn more fully toward others in love. Which approach shows our rootedness in Christ? Turning inward in protection or outward in love?

11

SONGS OF THE LORD IN A FOREIGN LAND

PSALM AND SONG

In the Psalms, we have a prayer book through which God puts us on the path of trusting in his promises.
  - J. Todd Billings

The roots of faithfulness often sink deeper in anxious, unsettled times. Faith can grow even — and sometimes especially — in the darkest of places.
  - David Kinnaman & Mark Matlock

I n one episode of the Canadian sitcom, "Corner Gas," the main character, Brent Leroy, plays a trick on his father, Oscar. Brent claims that Oscar has lost his Canadian citizenship and has accidentally become an American. As part of the gag, Oscar is asked to sing 'O Canada' at a local youth lacrosse game. To distract his father, Brent continues to sing lines from 'the Star Spangled Banner' every time he sees Oscar, telling him 'Remember you are Canadian, not American: don't sing *that*.' Filled with glee, Brent goes to the lacrosse game expecting to see his father sing the wrong song, only to learn that *he* is singing the anthem. Brent stands up and struggles. He sings one anthem to the tune of the other, then flips them. He has spent so much time singing the American national anthem, he can no longer easily sing the Canadian one.

This comedic scene unintentionally represents a spiritual challenge that Christians face. When we spend all our days hearing the songs of Babylon, will we know how to sing the songs of the Lord? Put differently, when our lives and days are shaped by the liturgies, habits, and patterns of our rootless world, how do we remain rooted in Christ? Do we run the risk of singing the wrong songs — with our lips and with our lives?

In this chapter, we explore the role the psalms play in the life of Israel, serving as an instrument the Spirit uses to root Israel in its identity during their time in exile. By singing and praying the psalms, Israel's heart is tuned to the kingdom of God. Regardless of what the world around them sings, they sing the songs of the Lord.

Recovering the psalms is vital for our growing in rootedness in today's world. The psalms provide a wider emotional range of prayer and singing than we usually encounter in many churches, helping us bring our whole lives before God. Singing psalms, hymns, and spiritual songs also serves as a foretaste of the coming kingdom, as God gathers his scattered people every week in worship.

SINGING IN A FOREIGN LAND

"How can we sing the songs of the LORD while in a foreign land?" (Ps 137:4). This question from the lips of the psalmist cuts deep into the exile experience. We are far from home, uprooted from the land of our birth. How can we sing songs that long for the temple of God, that speak of the delight of coming into his house, when the temple has been torn down and the people are scattered outside of the land? How can we sing of the joy of God's presence, when all we feel is his anger or, perhaps, our own fear that God has abandoned us? How can we sing of God's faithfulness when it feels to us as if all the promises have failed? How can we sing in a place like *this*?

"By the rivers of Babylon we sat and wept when we remembered Zion" (Ps 137:1). Ancient Babylon is a place of despair for God's people. Their captors want them to sing songs of joy, but they want to weep (v.3). They have lost so much. They have endured such suffering. Their prayers are not those of joy and laughter, but are birthed in pain and cry out for justice.

"Daughter Babylon, doomed to destruction, happy is the one who repays you according to what you have done to us. Happy is the one who seizes your infants and dashes them against the rocks" (v.8-9). Only those who have watched as the Babylonians seize their children and dash them can pen such anguished prayers. They can sing no uplifting anthems in Babylon, for it is a house of despair and mourning for God's people.

Babylon also seeks to strip God's people of their identity, to capture the hearts of God's people and conform them to *its* image. God's people are in danger of becoming people formed more in the image of empire than of God, in danger of finding their home more easily in Babylon than in Jerusalem. The siren song of Babylon endeavors to squeeze God to the margins and then, ultimately, either tame the faith or eliminate it altogether. Babylon can accept God as a badge for our personal brand, or as our lifestyle choice, but won't allow us to treat God as if he is Lord of the Universe.

How can rootedness in God be sustained in exile? We face the same question Israel faced in Babylon. As we have already noted, the spirit of Babylon has not died, it has just gone online. We now live in a digital Babylon, where the pressures to marginalize our own faith are mixed with the challenges of immense suffering in our world. The rootlessness and displacement of Babylon make many of the "hype songs" of Christian contemporary music ring hollow. While it is sometimes meaningful, cranking up the praise music in the car often makes our faith seem shallow or inadequate, particularly when we are overwhelmed by doubts, fears, and pain. We need faith that will face the world as we find it and yet help us to cling fast to Christ. We need faith that is resilient in the midst of doubt, that can stand under the weight of suffering and fear. When it comes to faith in the midst of exile, we need the real thing and not some 'super positive' knockoff that can just as easily appear on a motivational poster. If our *only* response to the horrors we see on the news, read in our history books, or experience every day is to be happy, to "have more faith," or to find the silver lining in everything, then we shouldn't wonder why such a faith is unappealing to many in today's world. We need a faith that can hold both joy and sorrow, both anger and laughter.

LEARNING TO LAMENT

The Christian faith is much deeper and wider and stronger than platitudes and quick answers. Growing rooted in Christ in the midst of exile is a call to draw deeper from the wells of the Christian tradition. One thing we need to learn is how to sing and pray. There is no better school of prayer than the one God himself has given us: the Psalter. The Book of Psalms — the songbook and prayerbook of God's people — is God's gift to his people living in exile.

The psalms engage both the highs and lows of life in Christ. They speak of betrayals, injury, and abandonment. They speak of deliverance, rescue, and forgiveness. They speak of times when God seems distant, as well as times when the psalmist tastes the sweetness of God's presence and longs for more. The psalms even question God's faithfulness and his actions, calling him to keep his promises. The psalms ultimately place all of life before God. These prayers are prayed in the context of the covenantal relationship between God and his people. The psalms are not simply psychological venting, but bring these prayers before the Lord of the universe. Even complaints within the psalms are a form of trust because the psalm brings these complaints before God, believing God is good and powerful to do something about them. With the psalms, we can bring all our emotions and needs before the living God because we believe what the Heidelberg Catechism confesses about God's provision and care, "God is able to do this because he is almighty God and desires to do this because he is a faithful Father" (Q26).

"How can we sing the songs of the LORD in a foreign land?" (Ps 137:1). God's people cannot be sustained in Babylon merely on a diet of uplifting music, inspirational anthems, or 'positive hits' (as my local Christian radio station once put it). This is, in fact, what Babylon demands. They want the songs of joy, but God's people cannot sing them. They need to learn to lament.

Chuck DeGroat defines lament in this way: "Lament, the ancient art of crying out before God, provides us with a means of honest and raw expression in times when our grief is too much to bear. It does not offer a quick fix or a tidy theological answer."[1] All three parts of this definition are important.

First, lament is "crying out before God." Israel is called, through the psalms, to bring its pain and anguish before the Lord. They are told where to take their pain. They are not left to deal with it on their own.

Second, lament is a means of "honest and raw expression" — often an uncomfortable form of prayer for those of us raised in Western churches. We censor our pain and doubts, believing they are too unsavory to bring before God. The frequent presence of lament in Scripture is a reminder that God is not afraid of such emotions or questions.

Third, lament does not "offer a quick fix or a tidy theological answer." We don't lament to solve the problem. Our lament is a cry for help from God, centered not in solutions, but in covenant relationship with God.

We need to recover lament in our churches. DeGroat is correct when he says that "For the most part, North American Christianity lacks a theology of suffering. We major in praise songs and minor in lament."[2] Recovering lament can be a way to re-knit the fractures so many of us feel within our life with God. If we are forced to be happy (or at least present ourselves as such) to be accepted in worship or in the church, then we must cut off significant portions of our life from the presence of God. If God only wants to know the happy and #blessed parts of our lives, what do we do with the rest of it? What can we do with so much of the hard parts of our lives? If we cannot bring our pain and grief before God, then much of what life in a fallen world looks like will feel unredeemed. Placing lament alongside praise can reintegrate our life lived before the face of God.

John Calvin spoke of the depth and range of the psalms by referring to the Psalter in a particular way: "I have been accustomed to call this book, I think not inappropriately, "An Anatomy of all the Parts of the Soul;" for there is not an emotion of which any one can be conscious that is not here represented as in a mirror. Or rather, the Holy Spirit has here drawn to the life all the griefs, sorrows, fears, doubts, hopes, cares, perplexities, in short, all the distracting emotions with which the minds of men are wont to be agitated."[3]

The Book of Psalms gives an "anatomy of the soul" because every emotion in the human soul is presented and called forth in the psalms. We must remember, though, that these emotions are not called forth simply to be displayed before the world or for some purely therapeutic end, but in order to have them brought before God. As J. Todd Billings notes, "While the Psalms reflect a very broad range of human emotions, it is not just a human book about human emotions. Praying the Psalms brings our whole heart before the face of God, reorienting our own vision toward God and his promises."[4] Unlike the purely positive and upbeat music of much modern Christian radio, the psalms run the whole gamut of human life and bring it all before the living God.

THE SCHOOL OF PRAYER

Through the psalms, God teaches us to pray. The psalms give voice to our heart's deepest joys and pains, but they also serve to shape and direct our prayers. Praying the psalms is both a comforting and jarring experience. One moment, we are comforted as the psalmist seems to be saying exactly what our hearts have been longing to say before God. "Truly my soul finds rest in God; my salvation comes from him. Truly he is my rock and my salvation; he is my fortress, I will never be shaken" (Ps 62:1-2). The next moment, the psalm takes us in a different direction, one that might not come as naturally. "How long will you assault me? Would all of you throw me down — this leaning wall, this tottering fence?" (Ps 62:3).

These jarring moments are places where the psalms can deepen and widen our prayers, as we will explore below. The psalms not only express our unformed prayers, but actually teach us how to pray. As Jonathan Wilson-Hartgrove admits, "I never knew how many enemies I had until I started praying the Psalms every day."[5] The paths of the psalms teach us how we should pray and what we should pray. A regular practice of psalm prayer will educate us in the life of prayer before God.

The psalms sustain God's people in their time of exile. While they cannot easily sing the songs of joy, they can still sing before the Lord. In doing so, they are grounded more deeply in God's promises and called to bring even the sorrows and pain of exile before the covenant Lord in prayer, seeking his face and his deliverance. "But however far we wander from the stability we were made for, children of Israel remember that our true home is in the house of God. The Book of Psalms is replete with expressions of our longing to accept the invitation to come home to life with God."[6] This experience of praying the psalms in exile is continued by the scattered people of God in the diaspora and by the early Church.

Psalm praying is also a hallmark of many monastic traditions, which have voluntarily entered into the deserts and gathered into communities in order to live as God's exiled people in a world consumed by the lies of Babylon. In the monastic tradition, rootedness in physical place, learning to pray through the psalms, and rootedness in Christ are all intentionally intertwined. "Stability of places makes possible a workshop where he can learn to pray. From the very beginning of the desert tradition, the Psalter was used as a school for instructing the soul in the language of life with God."[7] To stay put in a place, to stay put in the psalms, and to stay put in Christ are vitally linked. By learning to pray the psalms, we are brought deeper into life with God. "On what grounds do we, as Christians, join the psalmist in praying to God as our own covenant Lord? We can do so with confidence because the Holy Spirit has united us to Jesus Christ, and we pray as ones who belong to him."[8]

If you want to grow more deeply in your relationship with Christ and develop resilience for living in this digital Babylon, I can recommend no better practice than praying the psalms.

LESSONS IN SINGING AND PRAYING THE PSALTER

But how exactly do we pray the psalms? Some of us might be in churches where this is a regular practice, but many of us may not even know where to begin. In corporate worship, a psalm or section of a psalm can be read together as a prayer, sung as a song, or even read responsively (the leader and congregation alternating verses or parts of a verse). The psalms can be used as guidelines for learning how to pray, directing how we pray and the ends of our prayers.

Let's look at how this might manifest in personal prayer before we examine the importance of the psalms in the broader life of the church.

We have all had this experience — sometimes, we simply do not know how to pray. Something absolutely incredible and wonderful happens in our life and we long to pray and to praise God, but we cannot seem to find the words. We reach a moment when every day feels like we are taking another body blow, where we can barely find the strength to cry out to God, let alone the words. Grief and pain crash over us and threaten to pull us under. We desperately need to pray, but struggle to know where to begin. In these moments and in many more, the psalms are God's gift to us. The psalms are not only God's Word to us, but also God-given words we are invited to pray back to him.

I often talk with people who have prayed long for certain people or in response to certain situations. Weeks turn into months and months often turn into years. They continue to pray, but they begin to wonder whether God truly hears them anymore. They pour out their souls daily and seem to get no response.

In such situations, I often suggest that somewhere in their daily prayers, they include Psalm 13:

How long, LORD? Will you forget me forever?
How long will you hide your face from me?
How long must I wrestle with my thoughts
and day after day have sorrow in my heart?
How long will my enemy triumph over me?
Look on me and answer, LORD my God.
Give light to my eyes, or I will sleep in death,
and my enemy will say, "I have overcome him,"
and my foes will rejoice when I fall.
But I trust in your unfailing love;
my heart rejoices in your salvation.
I will sing the LORD's praise,
for he has been good to me.

Praying this psalm lets us name the questions we feel deep in our hearts, but have never spoken out loud. Praying Psalm 13 brings our doubt, our anger, and our pain before God. At the same time, Psalm 13 also leads us *from* a place of pain and questioning *into* a place of trust. It concludes with "But I trust in your unfailing love; my heart rejoices in your salvation. I will sing the LORD's praise, for he has been good to me." When we do not feel confident in our own words, we can come to the psalms with confidence, knowing these are words God has given us to pray to him.

Praying the psalms can also force us to pray in ways we would not otherwise pray. Many of us run through the same patterns in our prayers, asking for the same things in almost the same way every time. Though there is nothing wrong with praying for the same things on a regular basis, our prayers can start to narrow or harden over time. Even when we are not reciting a set prayer, it can begin to feel that way, because we pray virtually the same way consistently. By praying the psalms, we can broaden and deepen our prayers. By following the psalms, we can find ourselves praying in ways, guided by God's Word, we would not have prayed on our own.

If, for example, instead of praying Psalm 13, we pray Psalm 113, we can be brought along paths we might not have chosen to pray. We start with the open phrase ("Praise the Lord"). We can focus on the first word, "praise," and how praise is the fitting response to God and all his works, how it is good and right to praise him no matter the circumstances. We can even begin doing just that: praising God for what he has done, naming before him all his mighty deeds. We can focus on the fact we are called to praise *the Lord*. No one else and nothing else is deserving of praise — the Lord alone deserves all honor and glory.

We move to the next phrase ("Praise the Lord, you his servants") and pray for the church gathered in different places across the globe. We may also pray for that great and glorious day when we will all gather in praise before the one who is seated on the throne.

We can then go on to reflect on God's name in prayer, praising now and forevermore, the sun rising and setting (v.2-3). We get all the way to verse 7: "He raises the poor from the dust and lifts the needy from the ash heap." We then start praying for the poor in our neighborhoods and in our city, praying that God will stoop down to lift them up. We pray for those living in tent cities or slums. Perhaps we realize that we simply do not know anyone who is poor. We realize that we can pray for a category of people, but our prayers have no faces. We then pray for God to move in our hearts and lives to put us in relationship with the poor and needy in our community. We pray to know their faces and their stories, and that we may be able to show them mercy and see God lift them up.

We come to the end of Psalm 113 and pray for those who have been given children and a home. We thank the Lord for all the ways that he has answered prayer in the lives of those among us who long for children, but we also pray for those struggling with infertility, for those for whom this prayer has not been answered.

Just in the examples of Psalm 13 and 113, we can already see how praying the psalms opens us up to new ways of praying, leading us along paths we might not have travelled on our own.

SINGING TOGETHER

The psalms can be prayed privately and individually, but they are meant to be prayed together. We observe this throughout the psalms through the superscriptions. In our English Bibles, superscriptions are usually represented as a heading in italics at the beginning of the psalm. They include notations such as "For the director of music. With stringed instruments. Of David" (Ps 61), "For the director of music. To the tune of "Do Not Destroy." Of David. A miktam" (Ps 58), or "For the director of music. To the tune of "Lilies." Of the Sons of Korah. A maskil. A wedding song" (Ps 45). These directions are part of the original psalm and are actually listed as the first verse in the Hebrew.

Many of these superscriptions indicate who wrote the psalm (David, Asaph, sons of Korah, etc.). However, many also include directions for how the psalm should be sung. They often tell the tune or even the occasion for the psalm. While we do not have any of these original tunes anymore, the superscriptions tell us that the psalms were originally sung as part of corporate worship. They are intended not only for private prayer, but for the public worship of God. Psalms are prayers we sing together.

Though it is good to recover psalm singing (as well as psalm praying) in the church, it is worthwhile to note the importance of singing together in general. Worship is personal, but it is not fundamentally private. Sunday worship is not simply "me and Jesus time" that we happen to experience with other people in the room. Instead, worship is the gathering of the scattered people of God.

There is a taste of the end times in the gathering of God's people in worship. God's people were scattered in the exile and lived largely outside of the land. The church is scattered each week into all the places where God sends us in mission and service. Yet, each week we are gathered again into God's house. Each week we are brought home to find our rest in God.

Both in the Old Testament and in the New Testament, the great end times visions include the gathering in of God's scattered people:

> After this I looked, and there before me was a great multitude that no one could count, from every nation, tribe, people, and language, standing before the throne and before the Lamb. They were wearing white robes and were holding palm branches in their hands. And they cried out in a loud voice: "Salvation belongs to our God, who sits on the throne, and to the Lamb." (Rev 7:9-10).

At the end of all things, God's scattered people are gathered together in worship. Each week, when we gather on the Lord's Day, we enact, in anticipation, that great and glorious day. Each gathering in worship is a taste of the kingdom to come. It is no accident that in this gathering, God's people sing.

Joining our voices together is a visible sign of our invisible unity in Christ as his people. It is not a performance where a certain level of talent is required to participate. Instead, it is an act of lifting up our hearts to the Lord in worship by the power of the Spirit. We see a sliver of the kingdom to come when the people of God sing together.

Unfortunately, for many, gathering in worship is anything but an experience of the kingdom. Alan Noble admits, "I usually experience worship as an individual who just happens to be singing around other individuals. This sense is only heightened by the general lack of full-throated singing in many churches. Without delving too deeply into the worship wars, part of the challenge of contemporary services is that our focus is directed to the stage rather than to one another."[9] Instead of viewing our gathered singing as something that leads us together into the presence of God in worship, we can let it become an extension of our personal devotion time.

The presence of the psalms, along with the directions given in the superscriptions, point to a very different vision for worship. Worship — singing, praying, listening, eating, drinking, washing, sending — rightly involves the gathering of God's people together before the face of God in the house of God. Singing together (whether psalms, hymns, or spiritual songs) roots us in our shared identity in Christ. We are not simply individual believers who all have a personal relationship with Jesus Christ. We are the body of Christ, the bride of Christ, the fellowship of the faith. When we sing, we sing not alone, but together.

When Israel was sent into exile, they faced serious questions about how to live as God's people under the consistent pressures of Babylon. One of the gifts God provided for his people was the Book of Psalms. Including prayers of praise, trust, lament, and complaint, the Spirit used the psalms to root Israel in God as the Spirit taught them to bring their whole life before God in prayer.

A recovery of the psalms in the life of the church will help root the church more deeply in Christ in a rootless age. The same Spirit that used the psalms to root Israel in its identity when in physical Babylon can use them to root us in Christ when in Digital Babylon. The psalms deepen and broaden our life of prayer, but also call us into corporate worship, a fore-taste of the heavenly kingdom.

How do we live as God's people in a world that sings a different song? How can our hearts be shaped to love Christ and his kingdom when the rhythm of the world thrums every waking moment? We can learn to sing and to pray the psalms. The psalms offer more than a place of honest expression; praying and singing together constitute an act of resistance and counter-formation to all the pressures of Babylon. When the world calls us to place our self at the center, singing to the Lord restores us to our free and glorious place. When the world tells us to "suck it up" and "hustle harder," singing the psalms invites us to rest in the Lord and his promises. When the world tells us to hide the messy and confused parts of our hearts or simply vent them in outrage, praying the psalms invites us to place our whole lives before the Lord. When the world paints a picture of the good life as health, wealth, and fame, singing the psalms invites us into the kingdom of God, where God stoops down to lift up the lowly and seat them with princes.

Rooted in Christ, we can sing the songs of the Lord in a foreign land — songs of joy and lament, songs of trust and confusion, songs of anguish and of praise.

KEEP THE FEAST

THE LORD'S SUPPER

The Lord's Supper is a meal whose host is Christ.
   - Herman Bavinck

Communion with Christ was not simply a mental exercise. It was an experience of sweetness, along with aching for further union and communion with Christ, and communion with others.
   - J. Todd Billings

Some of the most important moments in life take place around the table. You might remember specific meals that call to mind the love, joy, and fellowship that happen around the table: a wedding dinner surrounded by friends, Thanksgiving with family, or a special breakfast at the diner with mom. Some meals stick firmly in our minds, but most of the meals we eat fade into the background. Yet, it is through the hundreds of meals eaten with others around the table that relationships often grow. It is through the meals we frequently cannot remember that we learn love, that we learn we will be cared and provided for, and that we learn joy in the presence of others.

Many of the most important moments in the life of God's people also take place around the table. Through weekly Sabbaths and yearly feasts, God shapes his people to learn his love for them, to experience the joy of his presence, and to be reminded of his care and provision. All these meals culminate in the Lord's Supper, the great feast of God's people, given to us by Jesus himself. In the Lord's Supper, God shapes us into our identity in Christ and draws near to us in intimacy. As we explore the power of the Lord's Supper to root us in Christ, we will look first at the biblical feasts that preceded it, then turn to the Supper itself and examine how God uses it in the life of the church. When we do, we will see that revival in the church may begin with a recovery of the Lord's Supper.

THE FOUR FEASTS OF EXODUS

When God leads the people out of Egypt, he gives them a calendar with seven feasts. Part of the process of unlearning the habits and desires of Egypt takes place gathered around the table. The calendar is a tool God uses to shape his people to set their hearts upon him.

In Leviticus 23, God institutes seven feasts that structure Israel's year around worship. The feasts include certain acts and rituals, but also specific meals or practices in family life. In addition to the yearly festivals, God gives Israel weekly Sabbath celebrations to further structure their time around the Lord. "There are six days when you may work, but the seventh day is a day of sabbath rest, a day of sacred assembly. You are not to do any work; wherever you live, it is a sabbath to the Lord" (Lev 23:3). The weekly rhythm of work and rest set the stage for Israel's life centered around worship of the Lord.

The first festival is the Passover. "The Lord's Passover begins at twilight on the fourteenth day of the first month" (Lev
23:5). The Passover, originally instituted while the people are
still in Egypt, is the feast of salvation, commemorating God's
rescue of his people from Egypt in the Exodus. In the tenth
and final plague, God claims the life of every firstborn in
Egypt, sparing only those who sacrifice an unblemished lamb,
paint the doorposts of their homes with the blood, and remain
sheltered under that blood during the night. God 'passes over'
them on the Passover and they are saved by the blood of the
lamb. It is no accident Jesus' saving death coincides with
Passover. We will explore more deeply the connections between
the Passover and the Lord's Supper later in this chapter.

Following the salvation feast of Passover is the purification
feast of Unleavened Bread. "On the fifteenth day of that
month the Lord's Festival of Unleavened Bread begins; for
seven days you must eat bread made without yeast" (Lev 23:6).
This second feast starts the day after Passover. Yeast or leaven is
commonly associated with sin and evil. A little yeast getting
into the dough will soon transform the whole batch. A little
sin entering into the life of a community will soon transform
it as well. Thus, the feast of unleavened bread and the removal
of all leaven from Israel is a seven-day period of cleansing and
purification. God's people must not only remove all yeast, but
also remove evil from their lives and their community.

The third festival is known as First Fruits. The priests of
Israel offer before the Lord the first produce of the land at the
harvest (Lev 23:9-14). The grain is offered as a "wave offering"
before God, accompanied by the sacrifice of a year-old lamb
and the presentation of a food offering of grain mixed with
olive oil and a drink offering of wine. God brought the people
into a fruitful land; accordingly, the first signs of that fruitful-
ness belong to God. Just as the firstborn sons and livestock
belong to God (Ex 22:29, connected with the Passover), the

first produce of the land also belongs to the Lord. They give God the "first fruits," trusting that he will give them more. Instead of taking care of themselves first and only giving what is leftover to God, they are instructed to give to God first and trust that he will provide for them.

The fourth feast God gives Israel to structure its time and life together is Pentecost (Lev 23:15-21). Also known as the "Feast of Weeks," Pentecost takes place seven weeks (fifty full days) after First Fruits. It is one of three feasts (along with Passover and Tabernacles) where all the people gather together for the festival. There are burnt offerings, grain offerings, wave offerings, and drink offerings. Yeast is now included in the bread offered before the Lord. Additionally, a goat is sacrificed as a sin offering and two lambs are sacrificed as a fellowship offering.

These first four festivals focus Israel's life around the time of the Exodus. The number of days from Passover to Pentecost in the yearly calendar corresponds to the time between the original Passover and God's people standing before the LORD at the foot of Mount Sinai, where they receive the Law. Every year, by keeping the feasts, the people relive the Exodus. They huddle in their houses as the angel of death passes over. They pass through the Red Sea on dry ground. They stand before God at the mountain. Each year, they remember. As we will see below, this remembrance is not merely recollection, but participation.

The first four spring festivals also connect with God's great work of salvation in Jesus Christ. The first Exodus is fulfilled in the work of Christ, so the feasts that draw the people back into the Exodus story are deeply connected with the Jesus story. Jesus was crucified as the sacrificial lamb on Passover. It is his blood that covers over his people. Jesus was raised as the first fruits of those who will rise from the dead (1 Cor 15:20) and ascended to the right hand of the Father so that the Spirit would be sent on Pentecost to write God's Law on his people's hearts. Salvation from sin through Jesus Christ follows the same path as the Exodus, which is the same path that Israel reenacted every year in its calendar.

RESTING AND FEASTING

The three other festivals are not as closely connected to the Exodus story, but still focus on God's work.

The fifth festival is the "Feast of Trumpets." "Say to the Israelites: 'On the first day of the seventh month you are to have a day of sabbath rest, a sacred assembly commemorated with trumpet blasts. Do no regular work, but present a food offering to the Lord.'" (Lev 23:24-25). Trumpet blasts are associated with liberty (Lev 25:8-10) and God's victory (Josh 2). The people celebrate God's past victory, but also anticipate the last day, when God's victory over sin, death, and the devil will come at the sound of the trumpets (Rev 8-11).

The sixth festival is Yom Kippur, the Day of Atonement. "Do not do any work on that day, because it is the Day of Atonement, when atonement is made for you before the Lord your God" (Lev 25:28). This is the most holy of days, when the offering is made for the people's sins. It is the only day the High Priest enters the Holy of Holies. One goat is slaughtered for the people's sins (Lev 16:15), while the priest lays hands on a second goat and confesses the people's sins over it, then sends it out into the wilderness to carry their sins "to a remote place" (Lev 16:20-22). It is the strictest day of rest during the entire year. Anyone found working on Yom Kippur is cut off from God's people. During Yom Kippur, the people are reminded that neither their activity nor their obedience could cleanse them from sin. All atonement is the work of God, not a work of human hands.

The last festival laid out in Leviticus 23 is Sukkoth, the

Feast of Tabernacles.[1] This feast celebrates God's provision of shelter for his people in the wilderness. Each year, God's people build temporary shelters (singular *sukkah*, plural *sukkoth*) and live in them during the festival. "Live in temporary shelters for seven days: All native-born Israelites are to live in such shelters so your descendants will know that I had the Israelites live in temporary shelters when I brought them out of Egypt. I am the Lord your God.'" (Lev 23:42-43).

This series of seven festivals, in addition to weekly Sabbath celebrations, structures Israel's life around the great events of God's provision and salvation. The Spirit uses the feasts to root them in the story of God's dealing with his people. The feasts are a liturgy that forms them as God's people.

Like today, Israel lived in a world with competing calendars. No, there wasn't a Super Bowl, a Valentine's Day, or an Independence Day. But the pressures were there just the same. The man-made calendar speaks falsely about the purpose of rest, about what is worth celebrating, and about the purpose of human life. Keeping the feasts forms the people around God in a world determined to shape them differently.

For the world, rest is simply a means of boosting productivity; it is not a way to honor God and rest in him. Egypt is a land of oppression and death, a culture that has no Sabbath. Egypt wants nothing more than to squeeze a little more productivity out of the Israelites.

This is not so different from how today's productivity gurus speak of rest — rest is not Sabbath, but a time to recharge for greater workplace productivity next week. In this kind of world, the practice of Sabbath is a gift and a means of counter-formation as God's people.

For the world, only human achievement or sacrifice is worth celebrating. We celebrate victories and losses, remember freedoms gained and lives lost. How we structure our calendars shapes us.

God gives his people festivals to shape them around the Exodus story, around his great victory and liberation. There is no day commemorating Abraham rescuing Lot from captivity (Gen 14), nor David's many victories over his enemies. These events are recorded in the Bible, but they are not celebrated as *the* events that define the people of God. God's people are defined by God's saving work, not their own activity or achievement. This is why many of these festivals come with the instruction *not to work*. This instruction is not only to allow people to gather and celebrate, but also to serve as a reminder of *who* did the work they remember in this festival.

For the world, the calendar is structured around our happiness and self-fulfillment. All holidays are essentially vacation days. Even the somber secular holidays have all been swept up in the desire for fun and leisure. Don't forget the sales. Whether the holiday calls us to remember the fallen, to lament our past, or to look to our nation's future, there will always be a sale.

The biblical festivals are different. Some contain celebration, some involve the expression of sorrow and some call for repentance. Like the psalms, the feasts encompass the full range of human emotion and bring it into the story of God's people.

Central to the biblical festivals are the acts of sacrifice and eating. Sacrifices of various kinds are consistently made to the Lord, and the people or priests often eat. They eat together and they eat with God. Tying together eating and sacrifice points to the great ritual of remembrance given by our Lord Jesus Christ — the Lord's Supper.

COMING TO THE TABLE OF THE LORD

The case can be made, on the basis of the seven feasts of Israel, that Christian churches should recover the church calendar.

Though the church calendar is not commanded in Scripture, the church has also sought to structure time according to the great events of salvation history. Like Israel before it, the church lives according to the rhythms and remembrances of God's work in history. The seasons of Advent, Christmas, Lent, Easter, and Ordinary Time, as well as the particular celebrations of days like Epiphany and Pentecost, reorient the life of the church around God.

However useful such recovery might be, I believe it is far more crucial that churches first recover the practice of the Lord's Supper. Revival in the church often coincides with a revival of the Lord's Supper. In the Scottish Reformed tradition, there was the practice of "holy fairs," large multi-day outdoor festivals culminating in the celebration of the Lord's Supper. These festivals included singing, preaching, and fasting, as people were invited to prepare their hearts for the feast of the Lord's Supper. These outdoor revivals ended not in an altar call, but in a call to come to the Table.[2]

Additionally, though the Reformation was a revival of the proclamation of the Word of God, it was also a revival of the practice of the Lord's Supper. While many Protestants today think that communion should be celebrated less frequently in order to keep it from becoming a "rote practice" without meaning, the reformers encountered the opposite problem. While Calvin and others simplified worship along more clearly biblical lines, they advocated for more frequent communion than we would find in most protestant churches. In contrast to the practices he saw in the churches, Calvin said, "It should have been done far differently: the Lord's Table should have been spread at least once a week for the assembly of Christians, and the promises declared in it should feed us spiritually."[3]

The recovery of the Lord's Supper was central to the Reformers (and should be to us) because God meets us in the Supper. He works through this meal to shape and nourish us, to commune with us and to ground us in hope. In this Supper, like Israel with the feasts, we remember the great story of God's work of redemption and, by remembering, participate in it.

Jesus commands us to eat and drink at the Supper "in remembrance of him" (Lk 22:19). This remembrance is more than just calling something to mind, like pulling up a memory on the video screen of our brains. Remembering is more than just thinking hard about the cross as we eat the bread and drink the cup. Instead, remembering at the Supper pulls us into *the* story of God's redemption in such a way that it becomes *our* story. As J. Todd Billings says, "Some "remembering" is trite — like remembering a shopping list; but other remembering is identity forming — opening up a new world, a new drama to inhabit."[4]

In the Passover, Israel retells the public story of the Exodus so that God will use it to make them participants in that story. Drawing on the work of Jon Levenson, Billings writes "With the sacrifice of the Passover lamb at the temple, and the celebratory meal of the lamb, unleavened bread, and bitter herbs, the Israelites did not move into private introspection (like many contemporary Christians do in remembrance); instead, they inserted themselves into the public history of YHWH's saving action on behalf of his people."[5] The history of God's actions becomes *their* history through participating in this meal. They don't look within to find out who they are, but look outward to what God has done. They are who they are because of God's work and they 'become Israel' in some sense through participating in this meal.

In the same way, the Lord's Supper rehearses the public events of God's work in Jesus Christ — his body broken and blood poured out on the cross for the sins of the world. In rehearsing this event through the Supper, Christians do not look within for their identity, but to the public event of Jesus' death and resurrection. "God's script for our drama does not originate from within, but in the history of Jesus Christ — his life, death, and resurrection. That is *our* history, as ones who belong to Christ."[6]

Jesus takes the Passover, which was done in remembrance of the Exodus, and tells us to do it in remembrance of him. He takes this meal that rehearsed the public events of God's saving his people and tells us to eat this bread and drink this cup, remembering the public events of God saving his people in and through him. "In taking these familiar symbols and investing them with new content, combining continuity and discontinuity, he is accenting the story of Passover in a different way and adding meaning to it that nobody had previously seen. It is not just that the Last Supper evokes the Passover in hindsight; it is that the Passover evokes the Last Supper in advance."[7] In the Lord's Supper, we remember in order to be drawn into the story of God's redemption.

The Lord's Supper is more than remembrance. It is also a feast of communion. At the Supper, we are nourished by Christ himself. As Calvin says, "Now Christ is the only food of our soul, and therefore our Heavenly Father invites us to Christ, that, refreshed by partaking of him, we may repeatedly gather strength until we shall have reached heavenly immortality."[8] In coming to the Supper, we are invited to the Lord's Table, where we eat with him. By the power of the Holy Spirit, we are brought into the presence of Christ, where he nourishes us and strengthens us for life in Christ.[9] Like with remembrance, "Communion with Christ was not simply a mental exercise. It was an experience of sweetness, along with aching for further union and communion with Christ, and communion with others."[10]

The Lord's Supper is not first and foremost something we do, but, instead, the gift of God for the people of God. It is an instrument through which the Lord brings us into the story of redemption and draws us into deeper union with Christ. While this spiritual communion with Christ is very real at the Supper, it is better felt than explained. As Calvin says, "although my mind can think beyond what my tongue can utter, yet even my mind is conquered and overwhelmed by the greatness of the thing. Therefore, nothing remains but to break forth in wonder at this mystery, which plainly neither the mind is able to conceive nor the tongue to express."[11]

When we come and receive the Lord as he offers himself at the Supper, we taste his sweetness. We experience the mystery and glories of his presence. We know him and we know who we are in him by receiving, eating, drinking, and feasting at the Supper. We come hungry to the table, are fed by Christ, and yet find ourselves longing even more for him. "We feed upon Christ, who brings life, and whose life in us by the Spirit bears fruit in acts of witness and love in the world; and yet, this feeding ultimately makes us more and more hungry."[12] As Paul calls, "I want to know Christ — yes, to know the power of his resurrection and participation in his sufferings, becoming like him in his death, and so, somehow, attaining to the resurrection of the dead" (Phil 3:10-11). We taste the suffering of Christ by eating the broken bread and drinking the cup. "Rather than a conversion experience, it is only in tasting the bitterness at the Supper — as an icon of bitterness in the Christian life under the cross — that we also taste the sweet fruit of pardon and new life."[13]

However, we do not eat and drink as those under judgment, but as those who cling to Christ and find in him our only sure hope of salvation. We eat and drink as those who know the risen Savior, who passed through death and the grave and entered into life again. "The triune God's love is not a spigot or even a fountain, but a raging waterfall that carries along his people as they are moved and sent into a world parched for life."[14]

In the Supper, our communion with Christ shapes us to live for Christ in the world. Christ *for us* enables us to live *for Christ*. Christ in us empowers life in Christ. "Feeding upon Christ comes first, and this leads to and enables communion with others in Christ, and an expression of the Spirit's new life in the world."[15] A revival of the Lord's Supper not only leads to deeper spiritual communion *with* Christ, but it leads to a life *for* the world.

The Lord's Supper is also a feast of hope. The congregation gathered around the Table on a Sunday morning is but a taste of the great and glorious day of the return of the Lord. On that day, all the saints from all the ages will gather around one table with Jesus Christ himself at the head. When we come to the table today, we get just a taste of that great marriage supper of the lamb. Because we will eat and drink bodily in the resurrection, it is vital to eat and drink bodily at the Supper now. The Supper is not a mental exercise, but an eating and drinking, a tasting and feasting on the gifts God has given to his people to nourish them in union with Christ. "If Jesus Christ is the one in heaven, and heaven will be an embodied feast and fellowship of love of those who belong to him, then the Supper as a foretaste should be embodied as well — involving touch and taste, the embodied fellowship of brothers and sisters in Christ."[16]

While there is great value in the church recovering the larger church calendar as a way of shaping the years of God's people, we will do well to begin by recovering the fullness of the Lord's Supper as we structure our weeks around the remembrance, communion, and hope we find in the Lord Jesus Christ and receive in the Supper.

INTIMACY AND FORMATION: THE GIFT OF THE SUPPER

In the biblical feasts, God shapes Israel by shaping time. By setting how they spend their weeks and years, God forms them as people who rely upon him and his saving acts, and not upon their own work and effort. The world's vision of time connects with its vision of what it means to be human, and with where we find security and peace. God invites Israel into a different way of being human, finding security and peace in him. In short, God teaches Israel to be rooted in him.

In the feasts, God meets with his people. The feasts often contain a meal that is both a meal together as a family (or community) and a meal with God. These are moments of intimacy between God and his people. Remembering God's saving acts is more than a mental exercise, but brings the people of God into the presence of God. Remembrance is tied with communion when God himself institutes the practice.

The Lord's Supper fulfills the promises of the feasts and ties together the threads of formation and intimacy with Jesus. The Supper unites us with Christ and with all the saints throughout the ages. In a world endlessly enamored with the present, the Lord's Supper calls us back to the past — to the life, death, and resurrection of Jesus Christ — and pulls us forward — into the promised age to come where we will sit at the marriage supper of the lamb. The Lord's Supper reorients our vision of time and space by uniting us with the saints of Christ across the globe and across the ages.

In *Disruptive Witness*, Alan Noble captures how the Supper forms us into people of the kingdom of God:

> It is hard to imagine an act more disruptive to secularism than celebrating the Lord's Supper. Every movement of the liturgy of the Lord's Supper calls us away from a distracted,

flattened, material, individualist, and secular view of the world. The reading from the Gospel grounds the sacrament not in mythology or doctrine but in time and space, and it runs us out of our presentism. We are joined with saints across two thousand years, hearing the same words and partaking in the same sacrament because of one God-man and his words and deeds...By grounding the Lord's Supper thoroughly in ancient history, our faith unsettles our complacency in the present. It reminds us that *now* is not all there ever was.[17]

Through the sacrament of the Lord's Supper, God reorients us to find our life and peace in Christ. Recovery of the Lord's Supper can only serve to strengthen God's people to walk well the path of discipleship to Jesus in this world.

The Lord's Supper also roots us deeper in Christ because, in the Supper, Christ gives us himself. Eating and drinking at the Supper makes us hunger and thirst again. Even Christians can go about their daily lives as if God is not really involved or present. We can act as if we have to make our own way. Then we come to the Table and taste and see that the Lord is good (Ps 34:8). The bread is broken, our eyes are open, and we find that our hearts burning within us at the presence and word of Jesus (Lk 24:32). Like those who have tasted a succulent filet mignon for the first time, we cannot go back to the McDonald's drive-through anymore. Our tastes have been awakened to something much better than we ever imagined. The things with which we had been filling our lives no longer satisfy us. We come to the feast and find such satisfaction in Jesus Christ that nothing else will truly satisfy anymore. Jesus makes all the cheap substitutes fall flat. Jesus satisfies us at the Supper, but does not leave us sated. The Supper leaves us longing for more.

This explains why the leaders of the Reformation fought so strongly against those who had been withholding the

Lord's Supper from the people — keeping the people from the Table keeps them from Jesus. If this is where Christ feeds us, where he meets with us around the Table, then keeping the people from the Table also keeps them from intimacy with Jesus. Giving them only an occasional taste (once a year, once a quarter) may be just as harmful, leaving them hungering and thirsting for months.

These days, most of our churches do not withhold the supper for theological reasons, but for what they refer to as 'practical concerns.' It is often considered too much work to have the Lord's Supper every week. Many fear it will just become routine (less meaningful) if we have it every week. But what could be more practical and more significant for the life of the church than intimacy with Jesus? When we leave the people hungering and thirsting for communion with Jesus but deny it to them, they will either languish or start going back to substitutes, even if they know they won't satisfy. There are obviously other means by which we can have intimacy with God — prayer, praise, scripture reading, and other spiritual disciplines — but to neglect or to deny one that Jesus himself has given us (and even *commanded* of us) is wrong.

The Lord's Supper is the gift of God for the people of God. "In partaking of the Lord's Supper, we mysteriously and spiritually, but all the same *truly* partake in Christ, which has a real effect on us and our spirits. The Lord's Supper is profoundly at odds with a secular understanding of the world, which has no space or even language for an event so miraculous, so meaningful, and so irreducible. By keeping Christ's command to take the Lord's Supper, we present a sign to ourselves and to our watching neighbors that there are truer, fuller ways of being in the world."[18] In the Supper, we are nourished and are witnesses to the provision and gracious love of God.

One of the ways we can grow more rooted in Christ in a

rootless world is to come to the Table of the Lord. Like the feasts given to Israel, the Lord's Supper teaches us to orient our time and, therefore, our lives, around God's saving work, rather than our own efforts and accomplishments. Eating the bread and drinking the cup draw us back into the public history of what God has done for us. His work defines who we are. We are those who can gladly pray to the Lord: "You have shown the fullness of your love by sending into the world your Son, Jesus Christ, the eternal Word, made flesh for us and for our salvation."[19] Our identity, security, and peace come from outside ourselves, not from within. They come from the public, saving work of Jesus Christ on the cross and at the empty tomb.

The Lord's Supper also roots us in Christ by being one of the God-given means through which we have intimacy with Jesus. We learn to find our life and our hope from Jesus by experiencing the joy and satisfaction we find in him. When we feast at the table, we not only remember what he has done in the past and will do in the future, but we are brought by the Holy Spirit into the presence of Jesus. Through intimacy with Jesus our hearts are awakened and we grow to hunger and thirst for Jesus.

Drawing together spiritual formation and communion with Jesus, the Lord's Supper is a powerful instrument through which God nourishes and shapes his people. If we long to be more rooted, more whole, more at peace, we will do well to begin by receiving Christ where he promises to give himself — at his Table.

SUCH A TIME AS THIS

WITNESS AND WISDOM

Here in our little village of Anatevke you might say that every one of us is a fiddler on the roof, trying to scratch out a pleasant, simple tune without breaking his neck.
  - Tevye in *Fiddler on the Roof*

Being in exile is a high and ultimately rewarding calling. There is beauty in exile.
  - David Kinnaman & Mark Matlock

I f you could pick any time period in history in which to live, when would you choose? Some people might want to witness the heroes, poets, and artists of history, to be on the front lines of great change in the world. Others might want to journey to a much simpler and more stable time than our own. Yet, when we look closer at whatever period comes to our mind, we discover that it was far more challenging and complicated than we might have believed. Those living through the early Church, the Renaissance, the Reformation, or a revolution all faced immense challenges. If opportunity and trial abound in every age, the real issue then, for each of us, is not *when* we wished we had lived, but *how* we will live faithfully in the time in which we actually live.

We cannot pick what times we live in. We can only seek to be faithful in the here and now. Christians seeking wisdom for how to live now, however, can benefit from looking back at how our spiritual fathers and mothers faced the challenges of living in exile. Though many of the specific circumstances have changed, the underlying challenges have not. We cannot wish ourselves back into a different age, but we can learn from those who have been there. Through the stories of Joseph, Esther, and Daniel, we can see the importance of wisdom and witness for God's people living faithfully in a foreign land. They each faced different challenges and made different choices, but sought, in their own way, to be faithful in the midst of trying circumstances.

THE MIXED LEGACY OF JOSEPH

Wisdom and faithfulness can take different forms depending on what is at stake. In the story of Joseph, we witness the considerable administrative skills he used to save people from starvation, but which also left open the door for later abuse and exploitation.

When thrust into exile, God's people consistently find themselves in vulnerable situations. Sarah and Rebekah both face peril when foreign kings take an interest in them. Jacob lives under the thumb of his wicked father-in-law Laban for decades. David flees to the Philistines, but the court officials see him as a threat to be eliminated, forcing him to feign madness to escape. In Egypt, the people of God face oppression and extermination at the hands of Pharaoh. Life in foreign lands often comes with the threat of disaster.

There is, though, another consistent pattern that we see alongside the vulnerability God's people experience in exile:

elevation. Though they have been oppressed and crushed, God's people are still brought (by God) into positions near to the heart of power. Nehemiah becomes a cupbearer to the king (Neh 1:11). Shadrach, Meshach, and Abednego are "set over the affairs of the province of Babylon" (Dan 3:12). Outside of Israel, they were never kings or priests. In Babylon, though, they are recognized for their wisdom and put into positions where God can use them for his purposes. These positions, however, come with the constant temptation to lose their distinctiveness as God's people or face the threat of martyrdom.

Joseph is a prime example of this pattern of vulnerability and elevation. Joseph, the beloved son, is cast down into the pit, and sold into slavery, into the house of Potiphar. In Potiphar's house, Joseph rises, only to be cast down again into prison. Then he is lifted up to the right hand of Pharaoh and blesses the whole known world. Three times, he is cast down only later to be brought out again.

By the end of the story, God has transformed all these evil actions, even the hatred and betrayal of his brothers, so that Joseph is a blessing to the nations. He is exalted to second-in-command of all Egypt and uses his amazing gifts to bring food to all the people of the world. His wise administration prevents starvation. Nonetheless, Joseph's identity and legacy are complicated.

The famine that strikes the world is so severe there is no food anywhere, except in the stores Joseph has gathered. Everyone spends all their money to buy grain from Joseph, putting immense resources in the coffers of Pharaoh. That works for one year, but there is still no food the next year. When the people cry out, Joseph offers a deal — livestock for food. The people take it, desperate again to avoid starvation. They eat, but Pharaoh now owns all their livestock. They survive for another year, but the famine continues. With nothing left but their land and their own bodies, they sell both to Pharaoh. They eat and eventually survive the famine — Joseph rescues Egypt from starvation.

As Joseph saves Egypt, though, he also enslaves them. This is what we find so troubling about the system Joseph put in place — though almost every part of it made sense when it was implemented, the end result is slavery. "As for the people, he made slaves of them from one end of Egypt to the other" (Gen 47:21). By the end of the famine, Pharaoh has all the money, all the livestock, all the land, and owns all the people. The system that Joseph set up has made all this possible. His efficiency as an administrator of agriculture and finance has culminated with the people no longer facing starvation, but enslaved.

This is the troubling and mixed legacy of Joseph, and why, as resident aliens, we must be mindful of the systems in place in the land where we live (even the systems we put in place). Joseph worked to save Egypt. Scripture gives us no indication that Joseph's motives were anything but good. With Joseph as administrator, this system of land slavery only amounts to a 20% taxation. Good and kind, Joseph works for the best of the people, even when setting up this system. Yet, it still ends in slavery. And when someone unlike Joseph takes his place, the same system — the same power that Joseph gave to Pharaoh — is used to enslave Joseph's own people.

Joseph's efficient administration saves and enslaves the people of Egypt, paving the way for the later enslavement and exploitation of the people of Israel. However, there is also a personal cost to Joseph in being placed near to power. He is lifted out of prison and made second in command over all Egypt, but at what price?

When Joseph is elevated by Pharaoh, he is robed by Pharaoh in fine linen and has a gold chain placed around his neck. Long before, Joseph's father had robed him with authority as a sign of his position in the house, with a coat of many colors, a long robe with sleeves. That robe was stripped off as Joseph was cast down into the pit. When Pharaoh later exalts Joseph again, he robes Joseph with authority as a sign of his position in *his* house. First, Joseph is robed as second-in-command of the house of Jacob; later, he is robed as second-in-command in the house of Pharaoh. Whose son is he now? Joseph has been exalted over the land of Egypt, but at what cost?

There is more. Pharaoh gives Joseph a new name, Zaphen-ath-paneah, a sign of his new identity in the Egyptian court. Pharaoh gives Joseph a wife, and not just any woman, but Asenath, the daughter of the priest of On, the chief priest of the Sun-god, Re, one of the highest religious positions in Egypt.[1] Joseph marries into the elite of the elite. Yet, he marries a woman who does not worship the LORD, who instead is the daughter of a pagan priest. Genesis 38 shows us the damage Judah endures being separated from his brothers and marrying a woman of the land. Will the same fate await Joseph? He has been exalted over the land of Egypt, but at what cost?

Joseph has two sons: Manasseh and Ephraim. When naming the oldest Manasseh, he gave this explanation: "For," he said, "God has made me forget all my hardship and all my father's house." (Gen 41:51). Joseph has not forgotten God, but he claimed that at the birth of his son, he has forgotten all his father's house. Will Joseph forget who he is and whose he is?

As Joseph steps higher and higher into influence in the land of Egypt, the pressure of "Egyptization" grows. The more he steps into Egypt, the more he is tempted to forget his homeland, to forget who he is, and to leave behind his identity as the son of Jacob, and become the son of Pharaoh. Joseph still calls Egypt "the land of his hardships" when naming

Ephraim, so he has not been fully assimilated into Egyptian culture. The pressure to do so is there, though.

Joseph has been exalted over all the land of Egypt, but at what cost? Will Joseph leave behind his identity as a child of Jacob, a child of the promise, and become a child of Pharaoh, a child of the world?

As Christians, when we step into the world, step into influence and step into places of power, we may find incredible opportunities to do good. We may be like Joseph, who fed the world and, in part, fulfilled the promise of Abraham that all the nations would be blessed through him. Joseph did incredible things — through this story, we see that, when children of God, armed with the revelation of God and filled with the Spirit of God, use their God-given talents in the world for the sake of the world, incredible things happen.

Yet, as Christians, when we step into the world, into influence and into places of power, we need to beware of the cost. For Joseph, it is a new robe, a new name, and new relationships that tempt him to forget who he is and to whom he belongs — to forget just what kind of land Egypt is. For us, the temptations will likely be different. In this new opportunity, this new job, this new relationship, what do we have to leave at the door in order to enter? Are there convictions we have to leave behind, so that we will be welcomed or accepted there? Are there pieces of our identities as children of God that we will have to surrender?

This is not to say that we should never go out into the world or explore new opportunities — far from it. Yet, we would be wise to recognize that the recurring temptations we face are similar to those that Joseph faced. We can easily be tempted to leave behind our identity in Christ when we step into positions of influence. We can readily be tempted to check our faith at the door in order to be respected and heard.

Remember who you are. Joseph was exalted over all the

land of Egypt, but at what cost? When God places opportunities in front of you, when you are called to step out of one thing into another, remember that you belong to Christ, count the cost, and do not forget all your Father's house.

THE SHREWD WISDOM OF ESTHER

Wisdom and faithfulness can take different forms, depending on what is at stake. Esther is faced with the destruction of her entire people and is forced to use shrewd deception to protect the people of God from annihilation.

It was 586 BC when the walls of Jerusalem crumbled and the people of God were carted off into exile. The Lord promised to one day bring them home — until then, though, they must live in exile. Never truly at home, they live as one small people amidst a vast, powerful, and pagan empire. It was one thing to follow God in a land where faith was supported, encouraged, and woven into the culture. It is a completely different matter to follow God in a land filled with the trappings, temptations, and pressure of pagan Persia. How do we live for God in the land of exile?

The people can stand out boldly — be radically different from the world around them — and then find the heavy hammer of the empire pounding them back into submission. They can assimilate, buying into the vision of the good life promised by the kingdom in which they lived. To do so, though, they will have to abandon their faith — abandon their king and his kingdom.

It was not only our spiritual ancestors who learned to live "teetering on an unstable perch in a hostile world."[2] The situation of Esther is not that distant from our own. We all face the challenge of living in the world, in the country, in the empire, while simultaneously maintaining our primary allegiance to God.

When Queen Vashti is removed for disobeying King Ahasuerus, a plan is hatched to find a new queen for the Persian empire. A contest is held, with all the beautiful young virgins of the empire brought before the king, to see who will become the next queen.

This is not a contest where women are seeking the heart of the handsome prince. In fact, it is not entirely accurate to even call it a contest. These young, beautiful women do not volunteer, but are taken from their homes. Taken. Note that every verb we have when describing these women is passive. They are gathered. They are taken. They are put in custody. These women do not have a choice whether to participate.

Even worse, these women are not allowed to go home when the contest ends. After one night with the king, they are brought to the second harem. There, they receive beauty treatments and, yes, they are fed and clothed. But there is nothing romantic about a harem. These women have been snatched from their homes and taken to the palace, where their only value is for the king's sexual pleasure.

Esther lives with her relative, Mordecai, in the citadel of Susa, the capital city of the empire. When the orders come for the women to be taken, the Jewish Esther is not spared, placing her in an awful situation. God's design and will for sex is that it is only to be enjoyed within the bounds of marriage, and yet Esther is taken and placed into the harem of the king. Not only this, she must prepare for twelve months to spend her one night with the king, who probably has only one thing on his mind. Even more troublesome, the king is a Gentile and an unbeliever. Her virtue as a woman and as a Jew is placed in incredible peril for no other reason than that she is beautiful.

Wisely seeking the aid of one of the king's eunuchs, Esther brings exactly what she needs for her night with the king. "The king loved Esther more than all the other women, of all the virgins she won his favor and devotion, so that he set the royal crown on her head and made her queen instead of Vashti" (Es 2:17). She is a Jew and now Queen of Persia. She becomes Queen because she pleases the king. Vashti's removal is a stark reminder to her, though, of how quickly she can fall if the king becomes displeased. At the order of her relative and adoptive father, Mordecai, she hides her religious and ethnic identity.

One of the king's officials, Haman, has a grudge against Mordecai and the Jewish people as a whole (stretching back to the days of King Saul). After he is elevated by the king, the wicked Haman plots to destroy all the Jews throughout the empire. He declares the day, seals an order with the king's ring, and sends it to the four corners of the Empire. "Dispatches were sent by couriers to all the king's provinces with the order to destroy, kill and annihilate all the Jews — young and old, women and children — on a single day, the thirteenth day of the twelfth month, the month of Adar, and to plunder their goods" (Es 3:13).

Alastair Roberts and Andrew Wilson point out how common, though wicked, Haman's plot is. "This move, from jealousy to hatred to attempted genocide, began with Pharaoh, but has tragically played itself out repeatedly in history, from Haman to Herod to Hitler."[3]

Esther learns of this destructive edict and is faced with a choice: she can remain silent and hope this calamity will pass her by, or she can risk her life by going to the king unannounced to plead for her people. She fasts and prays for three days and asks all her people to fast as well. "When this is done, I will go to the king, even though it is against the law. And if I perish, I perish" (Es 4:16).

Almost everything about Esther's life is full of chaos and peril. Her life is at risk, and her family's life, as well as the lives of her entire people, hangs in the balance. Haman, son of Hammadatha, the Agagite, the enemy of the Jews, has the king's signet ring and the king's power along with it. The circumstances surrounding Esther are a raging storm, but when she emerges from her three days of fasting, she is calm.

Though Esther is in a position of weakness, she demonstrates strength and stability. We are not told of her internal struggles, but what we see is a sort of shrewd wisdom.

After three days of fasting, Esther puts on her royal robes and enters the inner court of the king's palace. She enters dressed like a Queen. She does not barge into the throne room, but stands, instead, just outside the doorway, where the king can see her. When he does, he extends the scepter, inviting her to enter. Not only does Esther risk her life and come away unscathed, but by standing at the entrance instead of coming straight in, when she enters, she makes it appear as if it was the king's idea to have her there.

> The king said to her, "What is it, Queen Esther? What is your request? It shall be given you, even to the half of my kingdom. (Es 5:3)

Now is the time, right? Say, "Haman has issued an order in your name to annihilate my people. He even bribed you. You have to stop him." This is where Esther will say what she came for, right? The king promised her anything, up to half the kingdom.

No. Instead, she invites both Haman and the king to a banquet. What may seem odd at first is further evidence of Esther's wisdom. First, if Esther demands that the king stop Haman right there, she must tell the whole court that Haman has duped King Ahasuerus, which probably will not go over well. Second, Haman is not present. Even if she convinces the king, he will later confront Haman, where the snake may find a way to slither his way out when it is 'just the guys' talking.

So, Esther invites them both to a banquet. She mentions

Haman, as if he is an afterthought. However, by putting them both at the banquet, she forces a direct and immediate confrontation when she reveals the plot. Her actions work to place her in the greatest advantage when she finally pleads for the life of the Jews.

The King and Haman go to the banquet. They start drinking wine, so it's a fair assumption that the king is in a good and agreeable mood. He asks the question again, "What is it you want, Esther? Make your request and I will grant it, up to half my kingdom."

> Then Esther said, "This is my petition and request: If I have won the king's favor and if it pleases the king to grant my petition and fulfill my request, let the king and Haman come tomorrow to the banquet that I will prepare for them, and then I will do as the king has said." (Es 5:7-8)

Another banquet. Why? Does she lose her nerve? Maybe, but I think her last phrase gives us a hint that she had a plan in all this: "and then I will do as the king has said." Originally, she came weakly to beg the king for the lives of her people, but two banquets later, she convinces the king that it was his idea to give her what she wanted. By the second banquet, her demand will be in accordance with what the king has asked her to do.

At the second banquet, Esther reveals Haman's plot. Haman is hanged and the Jews are empowered to defend themselves against those who would hurt them. The people are rescued from the brink of destruction.

Esther is surrounded by chaos and peril. She enters the king's court risking her life, but, later when she has the king and Haman alone at a banquet, she is able to convince the king that everything was his idea. "Remove the dross from the silver, and a silversmith can produce a vessel; remove wicked officials from the king's presence, and his throne will be established through righteousness" (Prov 25:4-5). The wisdom of Esther is in knowing when, where, and how to speak from a position of weakness for the sake of others.

The difference between wisdom and foolishness is the ground on which we stand. Esther begins with prayer and fasting. She begins by remembering where she stands. Only in God's presence can she remember who she is and whose she is, so that when the storm comes, when she steps out into the court of the king, she can walk in the way of God.

THE FEARLESS FAITH OF DANIEL

Wisdom and faithfulness can take different forms depending on what is at stake. With only his own life hanging in the balance, Daniel refuses to bend and even courts martyrdom for the sake of faithfulness to God.

Like Esther and Joseph before him, Daniel is forced into exile and later elevated to a high place in the secular government. When the Babylonians sack and pillage Jerusalem, they also carry off all the "young men without any physical defect, handsome, showing aptitude for every kind of learning, well informed, quick to understand, and qualified to serve in the king's palace. He [Ashpenaz, chief of the court officials] was to teach them the language and literature of the Babylonians" (Dan 1:4). Daniel and the other young boys are part of an intentional effort by the Babylonians to assimilate them into the language and culture of the empire. They will have new names, be fed the best food, be given the best tutors, and, hopefully, be transformed into perfect Babylonian subjects.

However, Daniel does not go along with the plan. "But Daniel resolved not to defile himself with the royal food and wine, and he asked the chief official for permission not to defile himself this way" (1:8).

Daniel refuses to eat the king's meat. This is not about personal health, but about identity. Part of how God sets Israel apart from the nations is through how and what they eat. Certain foods are forbidden as a marker of being set apart as God's people. Even the food that is eaten must be killed and prepared in a particular way. It is likely that part of Daniel's refusal is that he cannot guarantee that the meat has been prepared according to God's law (and it is likely that it was not). For Daniel, this would mean eating food that is ritually 'unclean.'

Additionally, it is common for meat to be associated with religious rituals. Paul deals with this specific problem for Christians in his letter to the church in Corinth (1 Cor 8). Accordingly, a combination of concern for the ritual cleanliness and a desire to avoid participating in idolatry likely lead Daniel to reject the king's meat. His decision to consume only vegetables is about maintaining his faithfulness to God's Word and thus about his distinctiveness as someone who belongs to God in a hostile world.

Daniel escapes his first trial unscathed. "Now God had caused the official to show favor and compassion to Daniel" (Dan 1:9). Daniel, like Joseph before him, has the ability to interpret dreams and this elevates him in the kingdom. "Then at Belshazzar's command, Daniel was clothed in purple, a gold chain was placed around his neck, and he was proclaimed the third highest ruler in the kingdom" (Dan 5:29). However, Belshazzar is killed (in accordance with the judgment pronounced by Daniel) and a new king, Darius, arises in his place. Government officials with a grudge against Daniel encourage Darius to make a proclamation that "anyone who prays to any god or human being during the next thirty days, except to you, Your Majesty, shall be thrown into the lions' den" (Dan 6:7).

Daniel again chooses faithfulness to God and potential

suffering. He holds fast to his identity in God in spite of the pressures to do otherwise. He does not change his routine of prayer at all. He continues to pray to God and not to Darius. Though the king is dismayed when Daniel is caught, he upholds the law and throws Daniel into the lion's den. God shuts up the mouths of the lions and Daniel emerges unscathed. Then, those who have accused Daniel are themselves thrown into the lion's den, resulting in their deaths. The king responds by making a proclamation that people are to revere Daniel's God.

While Joseph's legacy is mixed and Esther is forced to use subterfuge to rescue her people, Daniel does not compromise. Along with Shadrach, Meshach, and Abednego, Daniel is willing to suffer and die for the sake of the name of the Lord. These four trust that God can rescue them, but their loyalty to God extends even to death. "If we are thrown into the blazing furnace, the God we serve is able to deliver us from it, and he will deliver us from Your Majesty's hand. But even if he does not, we want you to know, Your Majesty, that we will not serve your gods or worship the image of gold you have set up" (Dan 3:17-18). While God's people show wisdom and shrewdness when it comes to protecting the people of God (and even the nations) from harm, this is not out of a sense of self-preservation. When it is only their lives at stake, they are willing to risk any harm rather than dishonor God in any way. They will even defy the empire and the so-called gods that it served.

When the lives of others are in the balance, however, Joseph and Esther must play a much more dangerous game, attempting to hold fast to God while also working in and with the powers of empire. They work to protect others, even at great risk to themselves. Daniel's choices seem clear, but Joseph and Esther's are far murkier.

Sometimes the choices we face are as clear as Daniel's and sometimes they are as fraught with peril as those of Joseph and

Esther. Sometimes our choices have consequences primarily for ourselves and sometimes the impact of our decisions reaches far beyond our individual lives. We need wisdom to know the difference.

WEDDING WISDOM AND WITNESS

What can we learn from the examples of Joseph, Esther, and Daniel about living rooted in Christ in a rootless world? How do we live out our identity in Christ amid the pressures of the contemporary world?

First, Christians need to cultivate wisdom. While supernatural dream interpretation or beauty has occasionally elevated God's people to positions of influence, the people elevated by God have been consistently marked by wisdom. This sets them apart from their peers.

We live in a world drenched in information, but thirsting for wisdom. In every culture, there are aspects that God's people can affirm and other aspects they must reject. The work of wisdom is knowing when to say "yes" and when to say "no" to culture, according to God's ways and not simply as a matter of personal preference.

In *Faith for Exiles*, David Kinnaman and Mark Matlock define the kind of wisdom needed by Christians in this way: "the ability to compare the beliefs, values, customs, and creations of the world we live in (digital Babylon) to those of the world we belong to (the kingdom of God). And once we've made that comparison, to anchor our lives — including our use of technology — to the theological, moral, and ethical norms of God's kingdom."[4]

Wisdom empowers faithfulness in a secular world. We must see clearly where we are in light of the kingdom to which we belong. This wisdom strengthens Christians for resilience and, at times, resistance to the dominant narratives and values of the broader culture. We can resist being cast back and forth by the winds of the age by being anchored in Christ and his kingdom. Regardless of where the winds blow, Christ and his kingdom will be our north star, guiding us as we navigate the seas of cultural change. Our churches are wise not to seek primarily to *protect* our members (and young people in particular) from the world and its influences, but to seek to *prepare* them to navigate it in a wise and faithful way.[5] This requires cultivating the virtue of wisdom.

Second, Christians need to recover the full sense of 'witness.' The Christian faith is not always a strategy to "win friends and influence people." There have been times when God's people were able to influence the broader culture and empire, but they have just as often run afoul of them. For many Christians, 'witnessing' is synonymous with evangelism and may include good works of service that show forth the love of God. We 'witness' in word and deed, by how we speak and how we live.

However, the root word for witness in the New Testament — *martyr* — was understood by the early Church to describe a very different kind of witness. A martyr is not simply someone who truthfully speaks the gospel message to the world (as important as that is). A martyr is someone who suffers and dies as the Lord Jesus did, because of their faith in the Lord Jesus. This was what witness looked like for the early Church and still does in many parts of the world today. It means suffering like Daniel, like Shadrach, Meshach, Abednego, like Stephen, like the Apostles, like Jesus.

One of the challenges of "suffering witness" in our contemporary context is in identifying it. It has become a bizarre fashion among Christian groups in the West to cry "persecution" at virtually any and every minor inconvenience. Any time the nation or empire is less than fully supportive of every aspect of Christian confession and expression, we claim to be persecuted. This posture not only belittles genuine persecution and martyrdom, but often prevents our witness from being received when such opportunities for genuine witness come. When we cry 'wolf' at every shadow of difficulty, no one will listen when an actual wolf arrives. We hurt our witness by falsely identifying places of persecution.

As Christians, we suffer, but it is not always clear that we are suffering for our faith. Sometimes, we suffer without an obvious or specific explanation. At other times, we suffer not for Jesus, but because of our own wickedness or foolishness. As contemporary Christians, we are not unique in suffering for our wicked actions and then claiming persecution. Peter spoke to the same thing in his first letter:

> Now who is there to harm you if you are zealous for what is good? But even if you should suffer for righteousness' sake, you will be blessed. Have no fear of them, nor be troubled, but in your hearts honor Christ the Lord as holy, always being prepared to make a defense to anyone who asks you for a reason for the hope that is in you; yet do it with gentleness and respect, having a good conscience, so that, when you are slandered, those who revile your good behavior in Christ may be put to shame. For it is better to suffer for doing good, if that should be God's will, than for doing evil. (1 Pt 3:13-17).

There is a double danger when the church suffers for its own wickedness, but wrongfully believes it to be persecution. First, we injure the public witness of the church as the world begins to associate the church with acts of abuse, manipulation, hypocrisy, power-grabbing, or lack of integrity. Second, we also numb ourselves to the call to repentance. If I think I am suffering for my faith, I have no need to examine myself or come on my knees in repentance. I am right, they are wrong —

there's no need to look any further. False martyrdom cuts us off from the vital work of repentance and forgiveness that lies near the heart of the Christian faith.

Recovering witness is tied closely to the cultivation of wisdom described above. We need wisdom to see where we are, learn when to say "yes" and "no," and then have the resilience to stand firm, even in the midst of suffering. We need rootedness in Christ and a deep anchor in God's word.

When we know Christ and his word deeply, we gain the ability to discern when we must take a stand and even suffer for our faith, and we need to know what hills we will simply be foolish to die on.

Perhaps an example will be helpful: let's look at prayer. In our culture, religion is considered a private affair that should not affect our lives in the public square. We are implicitly told that we can go to worship on Sundays, but we shouldn't let it affect what we do on Tuesdays. As it was for Daniel before us, praying before meals (even in public settings) can be a subtle witness that we inhabit a different world, that we serve a different king.

Alan Noble notes, "Our society's broad assumption is that religious exercise belongs in our hearts, in our homes, or in our churches. It doesn't belong in a booth at McDonald's. Public displays of religion are more offensive than public displays of affection, which I think partially explains some Americans' reactions to Muslims who say their daily prayers."[6] If our prayers, however, become primarily a form of witness, instead of an actual prayer to God, then we fall under the condemnation that Jesus leveled against the hypocrites: "And when you pray, do not be like the hypocrites, for they love to pray standing in the synagogues and on the street corners to be seen by others. Truly I tell you, they have received their reward in full." (Mt 6:5).

This is when wisdom and discernment become essential.

Our prayer should be a witness to the world, but we should not pray for the sake of witness. When we sit down at a restaurant and pause to thank God before eating, the world will notice. Yet, if that is why we pray — so others will know we are the kind of people who pray — we cease to truly pray. In short, praying in public before meals is good, provided it is genuine prayer and not a form of performance. We need the wisdom to know the difference.

Alan Noble sums it up nicely:

> If our public prayers or any other public display of faith ceases to be primarily about the spiritual purpose — in this case, thanking God for his provision — and instead becomes about others seeing us be thankful toward God, then we have exchanged the thing itself for the appearance of the thing. Our motive ought to be gratitude to God, not seeking attention. But if we find ourselves actually avoiding public prayer because it feels socially awkward, or because it feels like we're imposing our faith on our neighbors, we need to be able to call that avoidance what it is: a capitulation to secular ideas of the public square.[7]

COMPASSION AS RESISTANCE

Lastly, Christians should recover compassion as a form of resistance. We bear witness to Jesus not only in our willingness to suffer for his name, but also in our willingness to serve others in his name. Our first response to the evil and suffering in the world should not be to try and explain it, but to respond to it with love and compassion.

Christians are called to protest and resist evil and suffering through acts of compassion. We must continue to engage in "compassionate actions as a lament that witnesses that things in this fallen world are not the way they are supposed to be."[8]

Though we should work to dismantle systems of oppression, evil, and suffering; and work to see a more just world, "The point of compassionate action is not to "change the world." It is to be faithful and to bear witness in word and deed to a different kingdom: that of King Jesus."[9]

As Christians, we act with compassion, not for the primary purpose of changing or 'saving' the world, but because we serve King Jesus. We serve a king who "raises the poor from the dust and lifts the needy from the ash heap," (Ps 113:7) and so we bear witness that we belong to him and follow him by our care for the poor and needy. The world may say that 'might makes right,' but we serve a king who reached out to touch and to heal the sick, to give sight to the blind, and to lift up those who were brought low. Our acts of compassion bear witness to our king. "Our restless prayers of lament go hand in hand with compassionate protest until Christ's kingdom has fully come."[10] Through compassionate service, we proclaim the kingdom of Jesus.

We do not choose the times we live in. Like Joseph, Esther, and Daniel before us, we must navigate the complicated landscape of life in exile. Joseph left a mixed legacy, as he worked to save the people of Egypt, but set up a system others would use to enslave his own people. Esther was forced into a position and risked everything, using shrewd wisdom to save her people. Daniel refused to bend, even when it might cost him his life, and was vindicated by God.

Their choices, and ours, are not always easy and clear. Yet, when the church cultivates wisdom rooted in Christ and in his word, we grow in resilience to walk in this world. Wisdom enables us to hold fast to Jesus and to witness to him, even when that calls for suffering. That wisdom gives us the strength to engage in acts of Christ-like compassion to lament and protest the evil and suffering that we see all around us.

A wise church is a resilient church. A resilient church grows deep roots and bears the good fruit of compassion and witness in the world. The soil of our society is not particularly well-suited for growing deep roots of character and Christian identity.

We began this book by exploring the gift and challenge of place. We saw the gift of limits and the gift of life centered in God. We walked with the patriarchs clinging to God's promise of home. We explored what it means to be rooted — committed to our cities, towns, and neighborhoods as places where God teaches us to love and live as his people. We need a new rootedness in our physical places as our technological world invites us to be everywhere and nowhere at the same time.

However, we also saw the dangers of place. We observed Israel rooted in Egypt, the land of death and oppression. We also witnessed how Israel forgot God once they entered the land of Canaan. In our lives, too, living rooted in our physical places apart from God is not a recipe for freedom and life. It is only when we are rooted in Christ that land and place can be received as a good gift from God.

God plants, but he also uproots his people — even us. He called Abraham out of Haran, took his people out of Egypt, and even cast his people out of the land. Yet, God called his people to find their home, their roots in him. Thus, the final fruit of God's planting and uprooting of his people is the New Testament mission, where God's people put down roots in the Lord in the various places where they live.

How do we develop roots in Christ in a rootless age, in soil that does not seem to offer what we need to grow deep roots? We do it in a number of ways. We do it when we are baptized — cut off and brought into fellowship with God. We do it when we bury our dead — mourning fully and yet having hope in Christ. We do it when we sing and pray together. We do it when we gather around the Table at the Lord's Supper. And we do it when we seek to grow in wisdom, for a wise church is a resilient church.

None of us can choose the times in which we live. In a rootless world, we long for a place where we find peace, rest, and belonging. We long for a place where we are known, loved, and even challenged to live more fully. Our longing, and God's promises, change how we relate to our current homes, our physical neighborhoods, and our fast-paced, digital world. My hope, through this book, is that you have grown more at home in the one who is your true home, Jesus Christ.

BENEDICTION

We planted a large garden right before our first child was born. Climbing beans. Lettuce. Potatoes. Carrots. Tomatoes. Peppers. Corn. We thought we would have the time and energy to weed it. How much work could a newborn be? All they do is eat and sleep. We were so naive.

The weeds soon took over the garden and choked out many of the plants. Friends visited us and spent hours weeding the garden, but they could only do so much. After they left, we could not keep up. By August, the plants looked sad and the weeds vibrant. The garden produced little that year and we felt miserable, discouraged, and exhausted.

The following year, we planted a garden again. While wearing a one year old in a baby carrier, we diligently went out every evening as the sun began to cool and spent fifteen minutes pulling weeds. By July, we barely needed five minutes to weed. The healthy plants had grown up and prevented the sun from reaching the bare soil where the weeds wanted to grow. Those early days weeding meant much less work later and a more fruitful garden.

Like the vegetables in my garden, God plants us in order for us to grow. Being rooted in one place is not simply for the comfort of not having to move (though that is nice). We are planted in the soil of neighborhoods, acreages, and city centers, so that we can bear the fruit of life in Christ in those places. Stability *is* important. A plant that is moved too often will not be able to grow.

Yet, weeding is important too. Removing what will choke out a plant and prevent it from growing is work. But it is work with the long view in mind. Weeding today will not necessarily mean better tomatoes tomorrow. But weeding day in and day out will create conditions where tomatoes grow and tend to grow well.

While much of this book has been focused on our roots, our rootedness in place, and, ultimately, our rootedness in Christ — my hope is God has been weeding the gardens of our hearts. My hope is that God has used this book to help pull up some of the weeds of self-sufficiency and false security, of isolation and distraction, of restlessness and rootlessness that choke out our growth in Christ. The daily work of weeding opens up space for us to grow more deeply into our true identity in Christ. Our roots grow deeper in Jesus and our leaves broader and more vibrant, when we are not distracted or deceived looking elsewhere for peace or a place to put our trust.

As you go forth into all the places where God sends you, may you grow in grace and in the knowledge of our Lord and Savior, Jesus Christ. May your roots in him be deep. May you rest in him. And may you bear abundant fruit for the sake of his kingdom — thirty, sixty, a hundredfold. May you do it all knowing that it is not by your work, but by his grace and the work of the Holy Spirit in you.

"So neither the one who plants nor the one who waters is anything, but only God, who makes things grow. The one who plants and the one who waters have one purpose, and they will each be rewarded according to their own labor. For we are co-workers in God's service; you are God's field, God's building" (1 Cor 3:7-9).

ACKNOWLEDGMENTS

Every book is a group project. In the months of writing, months of editing, and the months before publication, I received encouragement, feedback, and aid from so many. All errors and mistakes are my own, but much that is good in this book has been made better because of the contributions of others. I remain immensely thankful.

To the Reformed Church of Stout, who first taught this city boy about being rooted in the soil.

To Bethel Reformed Church, who welcomed and loved this immigrant pastor and his family.

To my early readers. Your feedback helped me clarify and sharpen sections of this book. Isaias D'Oleo, Nathan Longfield, Anja Noordam, Derek Noorman, Steven Rodriguez, Olga Shaffer, Tim Shaffer, Carol Vellenga, and Terri Wing all provided invaluable insights on early versions of several chapters. I cannot thank you enough.

To my design and production team. To Angie Koersen, who designed the cover; my father, Tim Shaffer, who provided copy-editing; and my wife, Olga Shaffer, who typeset the manuscript. You helped take words on a page and make them into a book we can all be proud of.

Finally, to my wife, Olga. Your relentless encouragement and confidence has been a balm to my soul. The love you and our kids — Elijah, Moriah, and Joanna — have shown me has truly been a gift from God. You patiently listened to me ramble for hours on end as I worked through the concepts in this book. You gave me courage to make this book a reality when I was filled with doubts.

NOTES

INTRODUCTION

1. Walter Brueggemann, *The Land: Place as Gift, Promise, and Challenge in Biblical Faith*, 2nd ed. (Minneapolis, MN: Fortress Press, 2002), 1.
2. David Kinnaman and Mark Matlock, *Faith for Exiles: 5 Ways for a New Generation to Follow Jesus in Digital Babylon* (Grand Rapids, MI: Baker Books, 2019), 20.
3. Michael S. Horton, *People and Place: A Covenant Ecclesiology* (Louisville, KY: Westminster John Knox Press, 2008), 270.
4. Horton, *People and Place*, 265.
5. See J. Todd Billings, *Remembrance, Communion, and Hope: Rediscovering the Gospel at the Lord's Table* (Grand Rapids, MI: Eerdmans, 2018), 27.
6. James K. A. Smith, *On the Road with Saint Augustine: A Real-World Spirituality for Restless Hearts* (Grand Rapids, MI: Brazos Press, 2019), 49.
7. J. Todd Billings, *Remembrance, Communion, and Hope: Rediscovering the Gospel at the Lord's Table* (Grand Rapids, MI: Eerdmans, 2018), 27.

1. THE GIFT OF PLACE

1. Sandra L. Richter, *The Epic of Eden: A Christian Entry into the Old Testament* (Downer's Grove, IL: IVP Academic, 2008), 102-103.
2. Brueggemann, *The Land*, 4.
3. Brueggemann, 3.
4. Hannah Anderson, "We Put Down Roots. Then Everything Around Us Shifted" *Christianity Today*, July/August 2021. https://www.christianitytoday.com/ct/2021/july-web-only/hannah-anderson-roots-place-shifted-home-pandemic-change.html
5. Richter, *The Epic of Eden,* 103.
6. Richter, 104.
7. Dietrich Bonhoeffer, *Creation and Fall: A Theological Interpretation of Genesis 1-3, Temptation,* trans. John C. Fletcher (New York: SCM Press, 1959), 49.
8. Bonhoeffer, *Creation and Fall,* 51.
9. Bonhoeffer, *Creation and Fall,* 51.
10. Bonhoeffer, *Creation and Fall,* 51.

11. Bonhoeffer, *Creation and Fall,* 51.
12. Bonhoeffer, *Creation and Fall,* 52.
13. Jonathan Wilson-Hartgrove, *The Wisdom of Stability: Rooting Faith in a Mobile Culture* (Brewster, MA: Paraclete Press, 2010), 72.
14. Wilson-Hartgrove, *The Wisdom of Stability,* 72.
15. J. Todd Billings, *The End of the Christian Life: How Embracing our Mortality Frees Us to Truly Live* (Grand Rapids, MI: Brazos, 2020), 143.
16. Chuck DeGroat, *Leaving Egypt: Finding God in the Wilderness Places* (Grand Rapids, MI: Square Inch, 2011), 20.
17. Bonhoeffer, *Creation and Fall,* 80.
18. Bonhoeffer, *Creation and Fall,* 81.
19. Richter, 111.
20. Bonhoeffer, *Creation and Fall,* 93.
21. Bonhoeffer, *Creation and Fall,* 93.
22. Bonhoeffer, *Creation and Fall,* 94.

2. THE PROMISE OF HOME

1. Brueggemann, *The Land,* 16.
2. Alastair J. Roberts and Andrew Wilson, *Echoes of Exodus: Tracing Themes of Redemption through Scripture* (Wheaton, IL: Crossway, 2018), 66.
3. Roberts and Wilson, *Echoes of Exodus,* 66.
4. Brueggemann, 5.
5. Heidelberg Catechism, Question 1 in *Our Faith: Ecumenical Creeds, Reformed Confessions, and Other Resources* (Grand Rapids, MI: Faith Alive Christian Resources, 2013), 69-70.

3. LOVE WHERE YOU ARE

1. Richter, *The Epic of Eden,* 33.
2. Richter, 37.
3. Wilson-Hartgrove, *The Wisdom of Stability,* 13.
4. Smith, *On the Road with Saint Augustine,* 141.
5. Wilson-Hartgrove, 25.
6. Wilson-Hartgrove, 25.
7. Smith, *On the Road with Saint Augustine,* 135.
8. Wilson-Hartgrove, 36.
9. Wilson-Hartgrove, 1.
10. Wilson-Hartgrove, 97.
11. Wilson-Hartgrove, 4.
12. Wilson-Hartgrove, 50.

13. St. Gregory the Great, *The Book of Pastoral Rule*, Popular Patristics Series 34, trans. George E. Demacopoulos (Crestwood, NY: St. Vladimir's Seminary Press, 2007), 171.

14. Eugene H. Peterson, *Under the Unpredictable Plant: An Exploration in Vocational Holiness* (Grand Rapids, MI: Eerdmans, 1992), 15.

15. Peterson, *Under the Unpredictable Plant*, 17.

16. Peterson, 20-21.

17. Wilson-Hartgrove, 40.

4. LAND OF FORGETFULNESS

1. John Calvin, *Commentary on the Book of Psalms,* vol. 1, trans. James Anderson in *Calvin's Commentaries (23 Volume Set)*, Volume IV (Grand Rapids, MI: Baker Books, 2009), 390-391.

2. Wilson-Hartgrove, *The Wisdom of Stability,* 114.

3. Wilson-Hartgrove, 124.

4. Peterson, *Under the Unpredictable Plant,* 11.

5. Herman Bavinck, *Reformed Dogmatics*, vol. 3, *Sin and Salvation in Christ*, ed. John Bolt, trans. John Vriend (Grand Rapids, MI: Baker Academic, 2006), 54.

6. Dante Alighieri, *Inferno,* Canto 1 in *The Portable Dante*, ed. and trans. Mark Musa (New York: Penguin Books, 1995), 3.

7. Peterson, *Under the Unpredictable Plant*, 1.

8. Alan Noble, *Disruptive Witness: Speaking Truth in a Distracted Age* (Downer's Grove, IL: Intervarsity Press, 2018), 38.

9. Billings, *The End of the Christian Life*, 86.

10. Noble, *Disruptive Witness,* 42.

11. Billings, *The End of the Christian Life*, 107.

12. Wilson-Hartgrove, 92.

13. Smith, *On the Road with Saint Augustine*, 100.

14. Smith, *On the Road with Saint Augustine*, 88.

5. GO FROM YOUR COUNTRY

1. Saint Augustine, *Confessions*, trans. Henry Chadwick (Oxford: Oxford University Press, 1991), 1.1.

2. John Calvin, *Commentaries upon the Book of Genesis,* trans. John King in *Calvin's Commentaries (23 Volume Set)*, Volume I (Grand Rapids, MI: Baker Books, 2009), 357. Calvin is commenting on Genesis 12:9.

3. Brueggemann, 6.

4. Brueggemann, 6.

5. Brueggemann, 21.

6. Horton, *People and Place*, 260.

7. Smith, *On the Road with Saint Augustine*, 5.
8. Smith, *On the Road*, 5.
9. Smith, *On the Road*, 82.
10. Smith, *On the Road*, 44.
11. Augustine, *Confessions*, I.1.

6. WANDERING BUT NOT LOST

1. Brueggemann, *The Land*, 8.
2. DeGroat, *Leaving Egypt*, 30.
3. DeGroat, 15.
4. DeGroat, 40.
5. Smith, *On the Road with Saint Augustine*, 66.
6. Roberts and Wilson, *Echoes of Exodus*, 41.
7. DeGroat, 63.
8. Roberts and Wilson, 48.
9. Roberts and Wilson, 61.
10. Smith, *On the Road*, 68.
11. Smith, *On the Road*, 70.
12. Brueggemann, 33.
13. DeGroat, 127.
14. DeGroat, 59.
15. Horton, *People and Place*, 293.
16. J. R. R. Tolkien, *The Fellowship of the Ring*, (New York: Ballantine Books, 1965), 325.

7. GOD'S SCATTERED PEOPLE

1. Roberts and Wilson, *Echoes of Exodus*, 110.
2. Roberts and Wilson, 113.
3. Kinnaman and Matlock, *Faith for Exiles*, 23.
4. Kinnaman and Matlock, 20.
5. James K. A. Smith, *You are What You Love: The Spiritual Power of Habit* (Grand Rapids, MI: Brazos Press, 2016), 41.
6. Kinnaman and Matlock, 24.
7. Kinnaman and Matlock, 26.
8. Dr. Martin Luther King Jr., from a sermon delivered at Temple Israel of Hollywood, February 26, 1965. Quoted in Kinnaman and Matlock, 19.
9. Kinnaman and Matlock, 25.
10. Kinnaman and Matlock, 27.
11. Noble, *Disruptive Witness*, 23.

12. Michael Hyatt, *Free to Focus: A Total Productivity System to Achieve More by Doing Less* (Grand Rapids, MI: Baker Books, 2019), 13. Kindle Edition.
13. Hyatt, *Free to Focus*, 14. Kindle Edition.
14. Noble, 11.
15. Noble, 27.
16. Smith, *On the Road with Saint Augustine*, 41.
17. Noble, 20.
18. Wilson-Hartgrove, *The Wisdom of Stability*, 137.
19. Wilson-Hartgrove, 137.
20. Kinnaman and Matlock, 35.

8. THE MESSINESS OF MISSION

1. Richard Bauckham, *Bible and Mission: Christian Witness in a Postmodern World* (Grand Rapids, MI: Baker Academic, 2003), 60.
2. Bauckham, 70.
3. Bauckham 72.
4. Emil Brunner, *The Word and the World* (London: SCM Press, 1931), 108.
5. Bauckham, 80.
6. Roberts and Wilson, *Echoes of Exodus*, 140.
7. Bauckham, 76.
8. Bauckham, 79.
9. Bauckham, 81.

9. CUT OFF AND BROUGHT IN

1. Heidelberg Catechism, Question 1 in *Our Faith: Ecumenical Creeds, Reformed Confessions, and Other Resources* (Grand Rapids, MI: Faith Alive Christian Resources, 2013), 69-70.
2. Nahum M. Sarna, *Understanding Genesis: The Heritage of Biblical Israel* (New York: Schocken Books, 1966), 131-132.
3. Jamie Ducharme, "COVID-19 is Making America's Loneliness Epidemic Even Worse," *Time,* May 8, 2020, https://time.com/5833681/loneliness-covid-19 See also the report from the Health Resources and Services Administration, "The "Loneliness Epidemic"" https://www.hrsa.gov/enews/past-issues/2019/january-17/loneliness-epidemic
4. Ben Cost, "Americans Have Fewer Friends Than Ever Before: Study" *New York Post*, July 27, 2021, https://nypost.com/2021/07/27/americans-have-fewer-friends-than-ever-before-study/

5. Tara John, "How the World's First Loneliness Minister Will Tackle 'the Sad Reality of Modern Life'", *Time*, April 25, 2018, https://time.com/5248016/tracey-crouch-uk-loneliness-minister/

6. John, "Loneliness Minister"

7. Wesley Hill, *Washed and Waiting: Reflections on Christian Faithfulness and Homosexuality* (Grand Rapids, MI: Zondervan, 2010), 97.

8. Hill, 115.

9. Dietrich Bonhoeffer, *The Cost of Discipleship*, trans. R. H. Fuller (New York: Simon & Schuster, 1959), 20.

10. Hill, 113.

11. Heidelberg Catechism, Question 69 in *Our Faith: Ecumenical Creeds, Reformed Confessions, and Other Resources* (Grand Rapids, MI: Faith Alive Christian Resources, 2013), 92.

10. BURIED IN HOPE

1. Heidelberg Catechism, Question 1 in *Our Faith: Ecumenical Creeds, Reformed Confessions, and Other Resources* (Grand Rapids, MI: Faith Alive Christian Resources, 2013), 69-70.

2. Smith, *On the Road with Saint Augustine*, 216.

3. Smith, *On the Road*, 210.

4. Noble, *Disruptive Witness,* 168-169.

5. Noble, 166.

6. *Worship the Lord: The Liturgy of the Reformed Church in America* (Grand Rapids, MI: Reformed Church Press, 2005), 106-107.

7. *Worship the Lord,* 31.

8. Smith, *On the Road*, 215.

9. Billings, *Rejoicing in Lament: Wrestling with Incurable Cancer and Life in Christ* (Grand Rapids, MI: Brazos, 2015), 48.

10. Billings, *Rejoicing in Lament*, 48.

11. See Michael Allen, *Grounded in Heaven: Recentering Christian Hope and Life on God* (Grand Rapids, MI: Eerdmans, 2018) 12-17.

12. Billings, *The End of the Christian Life*, 83.

13. Billings, *The End of the Christian Life*, 83.

11. SONGS OF THE LORD IN A FOREIGN LAND

1. DeGroat, *Leaving Egypt*, 133.

2. DeGroat, 32.

3. John Calvin, *Commentary on the Book of Psalms*, vol. 1, trans. James Anderson in *Calvin's Commentaries (23 Volume Set)*, Volume IV (Grand Rapids, MI: Baker Books, 2009), xxxvi-xxxvii.

4. Billings, *Rejoicing in Lament*, 38.
5. Wilson-Hartgrove, *The Wisdom of Stability*, 67.
6. Wilson-Hartgrove, 17.
7. Wilson-Hartgrove, 65.
8. Billings, *Rejoicing in Lament*, 51.
9. Noble, *Disruptive Witness*, 137.

12. KEEP THE FEAST

1. There is another biblical feast, Purim, which is established in the book of Esther as a celebration of God's deliverance during that time. Unlike the other feasts of deliverance, Purim is almost entirely celebratory.
2. Billings, *Remembrance, Communion, and Hope*, 45-46.
3. John Calvin, *Institutes of the Christian Religion, 1559*, ed. J. T. McNeill, trans. F. L. Battles, volume 2 (Philadelphia: Westminster, 1960), 4.17.46.
4. Billings, *Remembrance, Communion, and Hope*, 114.
5. Billings, *Remembrance, Communion, and Hope*, 115.
6. Billings, *Remembrance, Communion, and Hope*, 115.
7. Roberts and Wilson, *Echoes of Exodus*, 30.
8. Calvin, *Institutes*, 4.17.1.
9. When the Reformed talk about "Spiritual presence" at the Lord's Supper, it means that we come into the presence of Christ "by the Spirit."
10. Billings, *Remembrance, Communion, and Hope*, 162.
11. Calvin, *Institutes*, 4.17.7.
12. Billings, *Remembrance, Communion, and Hope*, 170.
13. Billings, *Remembrance, Communion, and Hope*, 131.
14. Billings, *Remembrance, Communion, and Hope*, 138.
15. Billings, *Remembrance, Communion, and Hope*, 148.
16. Billings, *Remembrance, Communion, and Hope*, 176.
17. Noble, *Disruptive Witness*, 143.
18. Noble, 144.
19. *Worship the Lord*, XXX.

13. SUCH A TIME AS THIS

1. Sarna, *Understanding Genesis*, 221.
2. Iain M. Duguid, *Esther & Ruth,* Reformed Expository Commentary (Phillipsburg, NJ: P&R Publishing, 2005), 3.
3. Roberts and Wilson, *Echoes of Exodus*, 118.
4. Kinnaman and Matlock, *Faith for Exiles*, 74-75.
5. Kinnaman and Matlock, 86.

6. Noble, *Disruptive Witness*, 112.
7. Noble, 113.
8. Billings, *Rejoicing in Lament*, 76.
9. Billings, *Rejoicing in Lament*, 76.
10. Billings, *Rejoicing in Lament*, 77.

Also by
Stephen C. Shaffer

Our Only Comfort: Daily Devotions through the Heidelberg Catechism

In a fast-paced world full of distractions, how do we create space to have conversations about faith? Parents long to talk about Jesus with their children, but are unsure where to begin. Families want to slow down and reconnect with what matters most, but struggle to squeeze anything into already busy schedules. Teens and adults desire to go deeper in their faith, but are filled with unanswered questions. In *Our Only Comfort*, Rev. Stephen Shaffer provides individuals and families with a helpful structure for growing in Christian faith. In a series of 364 devotions, *Our Only Comfort* will take families, young adults, and new believers through the core teachings of the Christian faith through the lens of the Heidelberg Catechism. Wrestling through questions like "Who is Jesus?" "How do I pray?" and "What does it mean to keep the Ten Commandments?" these short devotions create opportunity for conversations about faith between parents and children and provide nourishment for faith to grow.

Paperback: 978-1725298736
Hardcover: 978-1725298743

CPSIA information can be obtained
at www.ICGtesting.com
Printed in the USA
LVHW030616060922
727611LV00017B/113